SUPER SIX

The Steelers' Record-Setting Super Bowl Season

Pittsburgh Post-Gazette

TRIUMPH
BOOKS

When James Harrison rumbled 100 yards and somersaulted into the end zone after his record-setting interception return, he also tumbled into history.

This book is available in quantity at special discounts for your group or organization.
For further information contact:

Triumph Books
542 South Dearborn Street
Suite 750
Chicago, IL 60605
Phone: (312) 939-3330
Fax: (312) 663-3557

Printed in the United States of America
ISBN: 978-1-60078-297-8

All photographs courtesy of the *Pittsburgh Post-Gazette,* except where otherwise indicated

Content packaged by Mojo Media, Inc.
Joe Funk: Editor
Jason Hinman: Creative Director

Pittsburgh Post-Gazette
John Robinson Block, Co-publisher and Editor-in-Chief
David M. Shribman, Executive Editor and Vice-President
Susan L. Smith, Managing Editor
Mary C. Leonard, Deputy Managing Editor
Jerry Micco, Assistant Managing Editor

BOOK EDITOR
Donna Eyring, Sports Editor

PHOTOGRAPHERS
Peter Diana
Matt Freed
Lake Fong
Robin Rombach
John Heller
Andy Starnes
Pam Panchak

PHOTO EDITORS
Larry Roberts
Andy Starnes

RESEARCH
Angelika Kane

ADMINISTRATIVE COORDINATOR
Allison Alexander, Marketing Manager

contents

Introduction

By David M. Shribman, Executive Editor *Pittsburgh Post-Gazette*

This is how newspapers work, or at least how ours works: The newsroom is full of bright ideas, the editor has one dumb idea. Most of the time one of the bright ideas prevails. Sometimes the bossman's dumb idea does. But since my dumb idea for our celebratory issue of the Super Bowl championship never saw the light of day, I want to tell you what it was:

Hey guys, the dumb editor said by means of introducing his really dumb idea, let's have the Super Bowl headline read:

WORLD ORDER RESTORED; STEELERS CHAMPS AGAIN

I mention this not to display just how dumb I am but to say that this was supposed to happen—the Steelers were supposed to be sitting on top of the world, again—but it wasn't supposed to happen this year, or this way. It was way too early in Mike Tomlin's tenure, way too tough a schedule, way too weak an offensive line, way too improbable an undertaking for February 1, 2009. But don't dismiss that headline too swiftly. The world order has been restored. The Steelers are champs again.

This is the way the world is supposed to work. This is a reversion to the natural order. This is the customary way of business. God's in His heaven and all's right with the world. The Pittsburgh Steelers. Super Bowl Champs.

The book you hold in your hands is the predominant newspaper's way of saluting the predominant cultural influence in the predominant city in this part of the world. The Pittsburgh Symphony Orchestra is one of the world's best. The University of Pittsburgh and Carnegie Mellon are among the world's best. The Carnegie Museum is one of the world's best. The Pittsburgh Steelers are the world's best.

We're proud of our symphony—and of our ballet, and our opera, and our theatres, and all the community arts groups that give this city of grit its sense of artistic flight. We're proud of our flagship universities—and of all the smaller institutions of higher education that give this city of manual labor its intellectual lift and light. We're proud of our museums, and our libraries, and of the sandwiches and salads full of fries, and of Gus and Yia Yia Kalaris, who sell the very best ice balls in Pittsburgh and maybe anywhere, and of the cheese counter at Penn Mac, and of the sweets selection at Sarris Candies, and of all the little joints that sell fish sandwiches and pierogies and pizza so good that, if you pass Beto's on a cold evening, you will see people sitting in their trucks stuffing themselves in the parking lot. We're proud of all that, but when we talk of the noun pride the adjective Steelers almost always precedes it. Steelers pride. It's what we have, and who we are.

It was never so evident as it was the Friday after Barack Obama's inauguration—and 10 days before the big game—when the pianist who played with Yo-Yo Ma and Itzhak Perlman on the West Front of the Capitol just before the president's swearing-in appeared in Heinz Hall. Gabriela Montero's specialty is improvisation, and after she completed a bravura performance of Gershwin's "Rhapsody in Blue" with the Pittsburgh Symphony, she invited the audience to suggest a tune that she could use as a foundation for an improvisational encore. From about six directions in the hall came separate spontaneous roars of "Here We Go," the Steelers song—a tune the Venezuelan pianist didn't know. But within moments she spun those three syllables into a Bach-like fugue that won the biggest ovation of the night. PSO officials, mindful of the peculiar nature of Heinz Hall audiences, slipped the word to the next week's performer, Orion Weiss, who—silly man—thought he had been booked into Pittsburgh to play Grieg's classic piano concerto in A minor. Let me know when the Cleveland Orchestra does something like that.

Race back and look at this Steelers season and you will see—you will remember, because these are the things that defy forgetting—a remarkable tableau:

The two victories against the hated Browns. Jeff Reed's overtime field goal to give the Steelers a big 23–20 comeback win against Baltimore. The 11-play, 80-yard TD drive in the last minutes to defeat Jacksonville. The emergence of Hines Ward as a target of opprobrium for fans around the country and league. The Monday night victory against the Redskins engineered by Byron Leftwich. The five-game win streak that began with the only 11–10 final score in NFL history. The astonishing away-game victory against New England, fueled by five turnovers in five consecutive Patriot possessions. The 20–13 victory over the Cowboys that came as the Steelers scored 17 points in the final seven minutes. The interception returns by Deshea Townsend and Troy Polamalu that sealed victories against Dallas and Baltimore. The 4-yard TD

pass to Santonio Holmes with 43 seconds remaining at Baltimore to clinch the AFC North—a play sports fans are still disputing.

And then there was the Super Bowl.

Why we care so much about this event is no mystery. The professional game began right here. The coal mines bred great linebackers, the steel mills great linemen, the general environment brought forth a harvest of quarterbacks unlike any other, anywhere. (I'm old enough to remember Johnny Unitas, Joe Namath, and Babe Parilli, and the rest of you remember Joe Montana, Dan Marino, Jim Kelly, Marc Bulger, Jeff Hostetler, Gus Frerotte, and our own Charlie Batch, number 16, from Homestead.) It's part of our heritage because, well, it is part of our history. We own the Super Bowl because we own this sport's past. It is ours, and so maybe the old guy was right when he said that the world order had been restored.

Thanks for that goes to Ben Roethlisberger, Santonio Holmes, James Harrison, James Farrior, LaMarr Woodley, Ward, Polamalu, and so many others. Plus a coach who is a legend after only two years.

This is the sixth time Pittsburgh has won the Super Bowl. You know this, of course, because of all the six-pack talk around town and because one-for-the-thumb—the drive for the fifth Super Bowl, one for each finger—was only three years ago. Many years ago Harry Truman said he was in the market for a one-handed economist. (All the economists he knew kept saying, "On the one hand…on the other hand…") But in Pittsburgh we have a luxury. We need two hands.

So the new local slogan: Pittsburgh. City of two hands. We need two hands for all those rings. We need two hands to clap as often as we do. Three cheers for us. And then three more for good luck. Until next year. Seven Super Bowls will be almost heaven. ∎

Steelers Win on Holmes' Late TD Grab

Steelers 27, Cardinals 23 • Sunday, Feb. 1, 2009 • By Ed Bouchette

The Steelers not only have another Super Bowl victory to celebrate, it came in what might have been the greatest of them all, and they have another play and a winning drive for the ages to go with it.

Santonio Holmes caught Ben Roethlisberger's 6-yard touchdown pass, keeping the toes of both his feet in bounds as he stretched out along the sideline for the winner with 35 seconds left. It was Holmes' 40-yard reception with 49 seconds left that put the Steelers in position to win it on a drive that covered 88 yards.

And those were not the most dynamic plays of the game.

The final score in this super Super Bowl was 27–23, and it gave the Steelers their sixth Lombardi Trophy, the most of any NFL team.

"My feet never left the ground," said Holmes, the MVP of Super Bowl XLIII. "All I did was extend my arms and use my toes as extra extension to catch up to the ball. "We're going down in history with one of the greatest games ever played in the Super Bowl."

Holmes' touchdown catch saved the Steelers from what had been a fourth-quarter collapse at the hands of Arizona's Kurt Warner and Larry Fitzgerald. "Sixburgh" nearly became "Sicksburgh" as the underdog Cardinals stormed back.

Warner threw two touchdown passes to Fitzgerald to wipe out a 13-point Steelers lead in a span of five minutes against the NFL's No. 1-ranked defense.

Fitzgerald scored on a short pass that he turned into a 64-yard sprint up the middle with 2:37 to go, giving Arizona its first lead, 23–20. It came after a safety against the Steelers at 2:58 that cut the Steelers' lead to 20–16.

"I actually was thinking that if they're going to score, that's how you want them to score, extremely quickly as opposed to just milking it," said Steelers coach Mike Tomlin, at 36 the youngest coach to win the Super Bowl.

Up stepped Roethlisberger (21 of 30, 256 yards) to direct a winning drive in the final period for the sixth time this season—and throw his first Super Bowl touchdown pass.

The Steelers took over on their 22 with 2:30 left and were pushed back to the 12 by a holding call.

"I said it's now or never," Roethlisberger said he told his offense. "I told the guys all the film study you put in doesn't matter if you don't do it now."

They did it, especially Roethlisberger and Holmes, who caught nine passes for 131 yards, four receptions on the winning drive.

"I said to him that I wanted to be the guy to make the plays," Holmes said he told his quarterback on the drive. "Great players step up big time and make great plays."

Santonio Holmes' play throughout the winning drive will go down as one of the most clutch performances in Steelers lore. His touchdown catch to win the game cements his place in Steelers, and Super Bowl, history.

The furious fourth quarter came after what many believe was the greatest play in Super Bowl history.

Call this one the Immaculate Interception, because the 100-yard interception return by James Harrison helped deliver this victory.

Harrison's stunning touchdown on the last play of the first half turned the game around—until it was turned inside out in the final quarter—and it likely created a 14-point swing.

The Cardinals had a first down at the Steelers' 1 with 18 seconds left and were ready to take the lead or tie the score with a field goal on the next play. The Steelers led, 10–7, at the time.

Warner, fearing a blitz, threw a quick pass toward Anquan Boldin on the left. Harrison instead dropped into coverage, stepped in front of the pass, and ran down the right sideline for the longest play in Super Bowl history.

Harrison escaped a few tackles before he was hit just before the goal line. He landed on top of Fitzgerald, and they tumbled into the end zone. Officials reviewed the play, and it stood as a touchdown, perhaps the most astounding one in Super Bowl history.

"It was very tiring but it was all worth it," Harrison said. "I was just thinking that I had to do whatever I could to get to the other end zone and get seven."

Without that, the Steelers likely would not have won.

They moved the ball well at times, but had trouble scoring touchdowns. Twice, they had first downs inside Arizona's 5 and had to settle for Jeff Reed field goals of 18 and 21 yards.

The Steelers managed one offensive touchdown, a 1-yard run by Gary Russell in the second quarter that staked them to a 10–0 lead.

Warner threw three touchdown passes, including a 1-yarder to tight end Ben Patrick in the second quarter

and likely would have been the MVP had the Cardinals persevered. He was 31 of 43 for 377 yards with one interceptioin.

With 7:33 left in the game, Fitzgerald caught a fade pass for a 1-yard touchdown over cornerback Ike Taylor, who had held him relatively quiet until then. That brought Arizona within 20–14.

A punt later pinned the Steelers at their 1, and center Justin Hartwig's holding penalty in the end zone, by rule, cost them two points, making it 20–16.

Fitzgerald's lightning 64-yard touchdown came 21 seconds later and turned the raucous, overwhelming Steelers crowd deadly quiet.

The place erupted, though, when Holmes caught Roethlisberger's 40-yard pass to the 6 and the Steelers called their final time out with 49 seconds left.

Two plays later, Holmes made his incredible catch.

"I tried to throw it high, so he was going to catch it or no one was," Roethlisberger said, "and luckily he made a heck of a play."

The Steelers scored first on Reed's 18-yard field goal, but it was a victory of sorts for Arizona because the Steelers had a first down at the 1 and could do nothing with it.

On third down, Roethlisberger rolled right on a bootleg, trying to pass, and, with no one open, ran it in for a 1-yard touchdown. Referee Terry McAulay, however, overturned the call on Arizona coach Ken Whisenhunt's challenge and ruled Roethlisberger's knee had hit the ground before he got in.

Tomlin then opted to kick the short field goal on fourth down at the 1.

The Steelers did a better job of it the next time they got down there as Russell ran off right guard for a 1-yard touchdown behind fullbacks Carey Davis and Sean McHugh, who came in motion from the left to block.

That gave the Steelers a 10–0 lead, and the Cardinals over the past two seasons were 1–12 when they trailed by 10 or more.

Arizona, as it can, struck back quickly. Given plenty of time to set up as the Steelers rushed only three men, Warner found Boldin wide open and hit him for a 45-yard pickup to the 1. Warner's 1-yard touchdown pass to Patrick brought the Cardinals within 10–7 in the second quarter.

Harrison's touchdown changed the complexion of the game at halftime, giving the Steelers a 17–7 lead

instead of perhaps trailing.

In the third quarter, the Steelers moved 79 yards on 16 plays and consumed 8:39, but again they had trouble inside the Cardinals' 5. They had a first down from there and could not get it into the end zone. Reed kicked a 27-yard field goal, but safety Adrian Wilson stumbled into holder Mitch Berger for a penalty to give the Steelers a first down at the 4.

Three futile plays later, Reed came on and kicked a 21-yard field goal for a 20–7 Steelers lead. ∎

Hines Ward broke the big-game jitters for his team early with a 38-yard reception on the Steelers second play from scrimmage.

Though he ran for only 53 yards on 19 carries, Willie Parker managed to find enough daylight in the Cardinals defense to force Arizona to respect the Steelers' running game.

Team Statistics

	PIT	ARI
First Downs	20	23
Passing	12	20
Rushing	4	2
Penalty	4	1
Third Down Efficiency	4-10	3-8
Fourth Down Efficiency	0-0	0-0
TOTAL NET YARDS	292	407
Total Plays	58	57
Average Gain Per Play	5.0	7.1
NET YARDS RUSHING	58	33
Rushes	26	12
Average Per Rush	2.2	2.8
NET YARDS PASSING	234	374
Completions-Attempts	21-30	31-43
Yards Per Pass Play	7.3	8.3
Times Sacked	2	2
Yards Lost to Sacks	22	3
Had Intercepted	1	1
PUNTS	3	5
Average Punt	46.3	36.0
PENALTIES	7	11
Penalty Yards	56	106
FUMBLES	0	2
Fumbles Lost	0	1
TIME OF POSSESSION	33:01	26:59

*James Harrison's 100-yard interception return for a touchdown at the end of the first half ranks with Franco Harris'
Immaculate Reception as one of the greatest plays in Steelers' history.*

Texas Toast

For openers, it was a dominating outing, but the players aren't overly excited by the win

Steelers 38, Texans 17 · Sunday, Sept. 7, 2008 · By Ed Bouchette

The Steelers have become accustomed to winning season openers, yet rarely have they been so dominant in claiming their sixth consecutive opener by clubbing the Houston Texans, 38–17, at Heinz Field. They weren't perfect—Ben Roethlisberger did throw one incompletion in his 14 pass attempts—but their play yesterday rivaled the gorgeous weather that greeted their first game of the season.

"A beautiful day," Steelers coach Mike Tomlin said, describing the weather and his team's play.

"We're a good team, you know?" defensive end Brett Keisel said. "But I don't think anyone in here is going, 'Oh, yeah, we're so great, we got this big win!' All of us understand the schedule this year and all of us understand after each game we have another tough opponent ahead."

That would be the Browns in Cleveland, but for now the Steelers should feel good about reveling a little in the game they played to open the season.

Willie Parker, whose last season ended with a broken leg in game 15, showed off his renewed health and old form by rushing for 138 yards and three touchdowns on runs of 7, 13, and 4 yards, the most in his career and one more score than he had all of last year. Roethlisberger tossed touchdown passes to Hines Ward of 13 and 16 yards. Linebacker James Harrison got a jump on another Pro Bowl season with three sacks, and his new colleague on the other side, LaMarr Woodley, had a sack, an interception, and a fumble recovery.

The Steelers led, 35–3, going into the fourth quarter. Neither Roethlisberger nor Parker played in the final quarter.

"We're not going to overreact," said Ward, who led the Steelers with six receptions for 76 yards and had a long reception taken away by a penalty. "It's one game. We have a big game in Cleveland, prime time. We'll enjoy this, look at it. and get ready for Cleveland next week."

After Keisel and Casey Hampton stopped Houston quarterback Matt Schaub's sneak on fourth-and-1 at the Steelers' 48 on the game's first series, it was virtually all the home team until the fourth quarter. The Steelers scored touchdowns on their first three series: Parker scored twice and a Roethlisberger-to-Ward pass made it 21–0 after Woodley one-handed an interception and returned it 6 yards to the Houston 32. It was Woodley's first interception—pro, college, high school, midget—in his first NFL start.

"So far, so good," said the new left outside linebacker. "You have to bring the same attitude every week."

The only trouble Roethlisberger had on a day in which he posted his best completion percentage and a 147 passer rating came from Houston defensive end Mario Williams, who sacked him twice. The first came in the second quarter from the Houston 32 after Troy Polamalu's interception. Williams, second in the AFC with 13 sacks in 2007, hit Roethlisberger from behind and stripped the ball. Linebacker DeMeco Ryans

Ben Roethlisberger was nearly perfect in his execution in Week One. He completed all but one of his pass attempts for 137 yards and two touchdowns.

returned the fumble to the Steelers' 12, counting the 12 yards tacked on because Parker tackled him by the facemask. Such was the play of the Steelers' defense yesterday, though, that the line of scrimmage moved back to the 16 by the time Kris Brown kicked a 34-yard field goal.

"We really didn't stop ourselves," Roethlisberger said. "We had two sacks, small things, a little thing here, a little there. Nothing big. I don't think we made a lot of mistakes, and we didn't kill ourselves."

Even the Steelers infamous coverage teams contained Andre Davis, who returned three kickoffs for touchdowns last season. Davis averaged only 18.7 yards on six kickoff returns and Jacoby Jones returned two punts for 5 yards.

"I think that we played a good game in virtually all three phases," Tomlin said. "It was not perfect, but I liked the energy and enthusiasm from the people who went out and made plays for this football team," Tomlin said.

In the fourth quarter, Byron Leftwich finished up at quarterback and Rashard Mendenhall at halfback. Leftwich was 0-for-4 passing but Nate Washington nearly came down with one on-target, deep toss before dropping it. Mendenhall ran 10 times for 28 yards.

"I'm happy with the way we played but I'm not too excited," said Keisel, expressing the general consensus among his teammates. "I thought we should have won this game before we started."

They practically did. ∎

(opposite) Jeff Reed connects from 44 yards out for the Steelers' final points of the afternoon. (above) Troy Polamalu and the Steelers defense held Houston's offense in check all game. Polamalu also recorded his first interception in nearly two years.

Early Reign

High wind, rain keep both teams from effectively moving ball, but win puts Steelers atop AFC North

Steelers 10, Browns 6 · Sunday, Sept. 14, 2008 · By Ed Bouchette

Some things never change. Autumn follows summer, the Allegheny River flows into the Ohio, and the Browns lose to the Steelers. The Steelers won their 10th in a row against their longtime and close rivals, making it 16 wins in the last 17 games and nine out of 10 in Ohio since the new Browns returned to play in new Cleveland Browns Stadium. By winning 10–6 the Steelers took early command of the AFC North Division at 2–0 while Cleveland fell to 0–2.

It's as if the Steelers have a second home and it's in Cleveland, just a two-hour drive from Downtown Pittsburgh. "For whatever reasons, we feel confident playing here," said receiver Hines Ward, who scored the game's only touchdown on an 11-yard pass from Ben Roethlisberger in the second quarter. "Overall, we like playing in Pitt...Cleveland."

The Steelers beat the Browns in high wind—gusts were reported at 60mph—rain, and, on occasion, comedy. Cleveland blew a prime scoring chance at the end of the first half and then made a questionable decision in the closing minutes when Browns coach Romeo Crennel opted for a field goal instead of trying for the tying touchdown. The Steelers weren't without mistakes of their own, muffing a kickoff return almost as badly as it can be done.

But Roethlisberger (12 of 19, 186 yards) and Ward hooked up for their third touchdown pass of the season, and Jeff Reed kicked a 48-yard field goal to offset Phil Dawson's two field goals for Cleveland. Willie Parker also made it two games, two 100-yard rushing efforts. He ran 28 times for 105 yards.

"We're 2–0," Ward said. "Cincinnati and Cleveland are 0–2. They have to catch up to us. It is big. Everybody picked Cleveland as the team to beat. We came on the road and won up here, it speaks volumes for our team.... We are the division champions from last year."

It was such a game that the home fans booed when the Browns scored for the second time. It came when Crennel, on fourth-and-7 at the Steelers' 20, opted to kick a field goal with 3:21 left and the Browns trailing, 10–3. Dawson kicked it and the fans cut loose with their displeasure. The Browns still needed a touchdown to avoid losing, just as they did before the kick. But the Steelers used up all but 26 seconds on a long drive that ended at the Browns' 26 and Cleveland ended feebly when Aaron Smith sacked Derrick Anderson for the second time.

Roethlisberger and Ward hooked up for the game's only touchdown in the second quarter, and it came on third down and ended what was becoming a monotonous game between the longtime rivals in difficult weather.

The game was scoreless after the first quarter. Then Bryant McFadden intercepted his first pass of the season at the Cleveland 30 early in the second when Anderson underthrew Braylon Edwards. The Steelers drove to the Cleveland 40 after the interception and

Willie Parker went for 100 yards on the ground for the second straight game in the win over Cleveland. The win was the Steelers' 10th straight over the Browns.

faced a fourth-and-1 there. Parker picked up 12 around right end. Santonio Holmes (five catches, 94 yards) caught a 1-yard pass to the 12.

Ward then dropped a pass in the end zone on second down from the 11. Roethlisberger went right back to his veteran receiver on third down and Ward beat cornerback Terry Cousins badly, broke wide open into the end zone, and hung on this time for the score.

"To have that drop, to come back on the next play and call my number again, shows the confidence they have in me," Ward said.

The Browns strung together a nice drive at the end of the half, but in true Browns recent tradition, they muffed it. With a third down at the 12, Anderson sneaked 1 yard for the first down. There were eight seconds left and Crennel opted to try one pass into the end zone figuring if it failed, he would still have time to kick a short field goal. Troy Polamalu upset those plans when he made a diving interception at the 3 as time ran out.

"It sucks the wind out of them a little bit," Smith said of that play.

Browns fans loudly booed their team as it left the field at halftime.

The Steelers scored for the second time when Reed kicked his 48-yard field goal midway through the third quarter for a 10–0 lead. The Steelers moved into field-goal position based solely on one play. Holmes caught a 48-yard pass that Roethlisberger threw from the 16. Holmes had to fight off cornerback Brandon McDonald to catch the high and deep pass.

Cleveland finally scored with the help of two personal fouls on the Steelers defense. Dawson's 31-yard field goal put the Browns within a touchdown of the lead.

They would get no closer. ◼

(opposite) Parker could not haul in this pass from Ben Roethlisberger, but the quarterback played well despite his injured shoulder and the weather, completing 13 of 20 passes for 179 yards and a touchdown. (above) Hines Ward lays out for a pass. Ward scored the game's only touchdown when he hauled in a Roethlisberger toss midway through the second quarter.

Creamed by Philly

Roethlisberger is blitzed, bothered, and battered by Philadelphia's hungry defense

Eagles 15, Steelers 6 • Sunday, Sept. 21, 2008 • By Ed Bouchette

Ben Roethlisberger turned slowly around from his locker, his right hand wrapped with a white bandage but otherwise surprisingly unbloodied, and asked for a little room to operate. The gaggle of reporters complied. Too bad the Philadelphia Eagles did not.

Roethlisberger came under as heavy a pass rush as he has experienced in five NFL seasons as the rampaging Eagles defense sacked him eight times, injured his right hand, and sent the Steelers home with their first loss of the season, 15–6.

"We came out here and got the dog kicked out of us," offensive tackle Willie Colon said.

That Roethlisberger was able to walk under his own power out of this city was a small victory in itself. X-rays showed no broken bones although his hand was stepped on. Those eight sacks easily could have been a dozen if it weren't for penalties and a yard gain on several plays that negated more. Relief quarterback Byron Leftwich was sacked once to make it nine officially.

Philadelphia's pressure defense was the overwhelming difference in a close game. That pressure helped create two lost fumbles by Roethlisberger, an interception, a safety, and a meager 33 yards rushing, including just 20 by the NFL's third-leading rusher entering the weekend, Willie Parker.

"They took it to us tonight, no doubt," Steelers coach Mike Tomlin said. "They got after us. That's the story of this football game."

Tomlin said that as the game wore on and the Steelers (2–1) could not solve the problem, the Eagles (2–1) picked up steam. "There was blood in the water at that point," he said as the Steelers' second-half adjustments dissolved like papier-mache in a rainstorm. "They pinned their ears back."

"I want to thank our defense," Roethlisberger said. "They gave us many chances to win that game."

Roethlisberger completed just 13 of 25 passes for 131 yards and threw his first interception of the season. The Eagles threw a lot with Donovan McNabb completing 24 of 35 passes but just for 196 yards. The game's only touchdown came on a 20-yard toss to Correll Buckhalter.

Steelers Troy Polamalu and Bryant McFadden each had interceptions and McFadden recovered a Tony Hunt fumble. Tomlin was in no mood for moral victories on one side of the ball.

"I'm not worried about wasting efforts," he said of his defense.

At one point in the first half, the Eagles sacked Roethlisberger five times on seven plays and he lost a fumble on one of them. On the eighth play, Asante Samuel intercepted Roethlisberger's deep pass.

That's eight offensive plays, five sacks, two turnovers.

"We got our butt kicked, plain and simple," Colon said. "Obviously, we didn't do the job we wanted to come out here and do. We got lit up."

The Eagles moved readily on their opening drive to a first down at the Steelers' 25 when linebacker James Farrior stripped the ball from Hill after a short

Willie Parker had a tough day on the ground, recording just 20 yards on 13 carries. The dominant defensive performance from Philadelphia kept the Steelers without a win in the City of Brotherly Love in their last eight visits, dating back to 1965.

reception. McFadden recovered at the Steelers' 20. That led to the first scoring drive of the game, a 12-play effort in which Roethlisberger completed 5 of 7 passes and Reed kicked a 37-yard field goal. It was the only score of the first quarter and it was their only competent drive of the game until the end.

The Eagles claimed a 7–3 lead on a 13-play drive that ended when Buckhalter caught a short pass from McNabb.

The Eagles blitzed Roethlisberger hard and often and it paid off in the second quarter when they sacked him three times in five plays. Roethlisberger fumbled on the last one and Eagles tackle Brodrick Bunkley recovered at the Steelers' 45. That fumble led to a David Akers' 31-yard field goal and a 10–3 Eagles lead with 2:36 left in the second quarter.

Reed made the longest field goal of his career from 53 yards after McFadden's interception near midfield. That left the Eagles with a 10–6 halftime lead.

Nothing happened to change that until the Eagles recorded a safety in the fourth quarter when, under pressure and going down in his end zone, Roethlisberger tried to flip a pass to Mewelde Moore and was penalized for intentional grounding. Because the penalty occurred in the end zone, it was ruled a safety and upped Philadelphia's lead to 12–6 with eight minutes left.

A leaping sack of Roethlisberger on the next series by safety Brian Dawkins knocked the ball out of his hands. Dawkins recovered and Akers eventually kicked another 31-yard field goal for a 15–6 lead.

Leftwich came on and, against no blitz, guided the Steelers to the Eagles' 22 where the drive ended on fourth down.

The problem for the Steelers now is not so much what the Eagles did, but what every other defense will try to do, starting with Baltimore in their next game. "It has to be correctable," Colon said. "Any team that watches this tape right now is going to understand we're suffering with the blitz coming at us and if we don't get it done, they're going to blitz the hell out of us." ■

(opposite) Philadelphia's DeSean Jackson is wrestled to the turf. The impressive rookie had five catches for 40 yards.
(above) Ben Roethlisberger looks to avoid the Eagles pass rush. He was sacked eight times on the day as the Philadelphia defense crashed in for nine total sacks.

Turning Points

Roethlisberger expresses anger at half, sparks team to two quick scores; Reed kicks 46-yarder to win

Steelers 23, Ravens 20 (OT) · Monday, Sept. 29, 2008 · By Ed Bouchette

A burst of anger at halftime from quarterback Ben Roethlisberger at his teammates was followed by a burst of scoring late in the third quarter that boosted the Steelers from behind, and they beat the surprising Baltimore Ravens, 23–20, on Jeff Reed's third field goal of the game, from 46 yards in overtime last night. Baltimore players celebrated because they thought Reed's field goal went wide, but it hooked just inside the left upright for the seventh winning field goal of his career.

"Oh, yeah, there was doubt," Reed said as he watched the ball hook to the left.

The Ravens had tied the score with four minutes left when Le'Ron McClain ran 2 yards for their only score in the second half.

The Steelers were left with one running back, Mewelde Moore, for most of the fourth quarter and overtime after Rashard Mendenhall fractured his shoulder and Carey Davis sprained his ankle. Mendenhall, making his first pro start, will miss the rest of the season.

Moore did not let them down. He turned a short pass into a 24-yard gain to Baltimore's 31 on third down, keeping their winning drive alive. He then caught a crucial 7-yard pass on third down to put Reed in better range from 46 yards.

"To make a play to help my team out...I can't explain it," Moore said. "That [24-yarder] was the biggest play in my life."

The victory boosted the Steelers back atop the AFC North Division at 3–1. Baltimore fell to 2–1. "We're never going to quit," Roethlisberger said after the game.

He said something entirely different at halftime. The Steelers trailed, 13–3, and they were booed as they left the field. Roethlisberger shouted at his offensive teammates in the locker room. "I was tired of being booed," he said. "I was tired of being embarrassed."

Tackle Willie Colon said: "He's just being a leader. He said you either step up or die, and everyone got it in their minds they were going to fight."

Whether it was those fighting words or something else, the Steelers stunning turnaround late in the third quarter occurred within 15 seconds when it appeared nothing could go right for their offense.

Then something did go right.

"We knew we had to get jump-started with a big play or a turnover," linebacker Larry Foote said.

They got both. On third down, Roethlisberger threw a pass over the middle to Santonio Holmes for a 38-yard touchdown. On the next play, James Harrison sacked Ravens rookie quarterback Joe Flacco, who fumbled. Linebacker LaMarr Woodley recovered and took it 7 yards for a touchdown.

"I'd rather take the sack-fumble all day," Harrison said about Woodley's touchdown off his effort. "He can score all he wants."

Those two scores not only breathed life into the

Santonio Holmes races to the end zone to pull the Steelers within three points in the third quarter. LaMarr Woodley put the Steelers in front just 15 seconds later with his fumble return.

Steelers, but they also gave them a 17–13 lead in a game in which they looked ripe for an upset loss to their bitter rivals from Baltimore.

Roethlisberger had a rough time of it until then. He was sacked three times in the first half and threw an interception that helped the Ravens turn an early tide and their first score, the ball slipping out of his hand. It did not silence Roethlisberger, though, either in the locker room at halftime or back out on the field. He was not sacked in the second half and, using the no-huddle, found Holmes streaking across the middle on third down. He caught it behind diving corner-back Fabian Washington, then cornerback Chris McAlister missed a tackle, and Holmes completed a 38-yard touchdown.

The Steelers trailed, 13–10, with 4:09 left in the third quarter. One play and 15 seconds later, they took the lead at 17–13. On first down, Harrison hit Flacco from behind and he fumbled. Woodley fell on it at the 7, got up and ran into the end zone for a touchdown with 3:54 to go.

Their next drive came up 1 yard short for a touch-down, Reed instead kicking from 19 yards for a 20–13 lead. One play put them in scoring position. The Ravens blitzed six men on second down and Roethlisberger escaped it, shaking off linebacker Bart Scott to throw deep to Hines Ward, who was wide open for a 49-yard gain to the 10.

Baltimore, though, tied it, 20–20, when McClain ran 2 yards for a touchdown with 4:02 left. Regulation ended, and then Baltimore won the coin toss and elected to receive. A holding penalty on the kickoff gave Baltimore the ball on its 15. Lawrence Timmons ended that series with a sack of Flacco back to the 12.

The Steelers took over after the punt at their 43 to open the winning drive. They moved 29 yards on seven plays to set up Reed's winner.

"I knew we were going to get in my range," Reed said. ■

(opposite) Evading tacklers in the open field, Hines Ward looks for daylight. This catch went for 49 yards and was the game's longest play from scrimmage. (above) Steady in the pocket, Ben Roethlisberger completed 14 of 24 passes for 191 yards with one touchdown and one interception. The win was the Steelers' 14th straight at home on Monday Night Football.

Ben Roethlisberger

Big Ben produces his own drive

By Gene Collier

Not to be smug about it or anything, but I had no doubt the Steelers could go 92 desperate yards against the Ravens' defense.

None.

I just thought it might take 92 plays. Spread over two seasons.

"The best thing about this offense," Nate Washington said in the locker room of the 2008 AFC North Division champions, "is that we forget."

That happens to be too true. In what was perhaps as great a triumph of selective amnesia as of athletic heroism, the Steelers behind Ben Roethlisberger repressed their collective memory of the game's first 56 1/2 minutes and carved out a monument to themselves.

Washington forgot that he dropped two passes and had his hands on a third that would not have been a terribly remarkable catch. Santonio Holmes forgot that he dropped one right in his belly, that he fumbled another right into the hands of Baltimore's Ed Reed, that he had played most of 60 minutes as though he had no fingers and few clues. And Big Ben forgot those things, too, throwing with typical bravado at his two least reliable wideouts six times in the final 3:36.

It's a matter of NFL orthodoxy, if not actual copyright law, that "The Drive" belongs to John Elway, the Denver legend who is Roethlisberger's idol, the reason he wears No. 7. "The Drive" was Elway's masterpiece, the precise dimensions being 15 plays, 98 yards, in 5:02 to pull the Broncos into a tie with Cleveland January 11, 1987. The touchdown came with 37 seconds left.

But this is about Ben's Drive: 12 plays, 92 yards in 2:53 to beat Baltimore, 13–9. He went 7 for 11 (including a spike) for 88 yards. The touchdown came with 43 seconds remaining.

"Seven delivered," said an emotional Mike Tomlin of his Elway. "He's done it time and time again. A lot's been said of our offensive struggles, but when we need a play, when we have to move it, we have. Against San Diego, last weekend [against Dallas], and now today."

So brilliant were both defenses yesterday, and for most of this season, that it appeared the Steelers and Ravens could play until St. Patrick's Day without scoring a touchdown. In what might have appeared an interminable tug-of-bore to the untrained eye, the teams collected only five field goals over the majority of three hours, and Baltimore led, 9–6, when Mewelde Moore made a fair catch of Baltimore's seventh punt at the Steelers' 8 with 3:36 to go.

It was the fifth time the Steelers would start inside their 10, and if anyone in the huddle of white shirts thought they had 92 yards in them against a defense that had allowed exactly one touchdown in the previous 15 quarters, no one was saying it out loud.

"We were just sayin', you know, 'Keep workin',''' said right tackle Willie Colon, part of an embattled offensive line that kept Roethlisberger essentially untouched in the final minutes. "But look, if you don't believe, it's pointless to go out there."

Having now played five professional seasons, Ben Roethlisberger is hardly the new kid on the block. His 51 wins over his first five years is the most by any NFL quarterback during his first five years.

Ben's Drive started with a crossing pattern to Hines Ward, who made a great fingertip catch for 13 yards with Corey Ivy hanging on him like purple drapes. Ward caught another 13-yarder on the next play. It was first-and-10 at the 34.

Ben threw incomplete to Washington, and then to Holmes, but on third down, with Heath Miller inexplicably on the sideline and Limas Sweed inexplicably not, Roethlisberger threw hard into the left flat at Washington, who was going to be tackled short of the first-down marker until Reed fell down in front of him. It was first-and-10 at the 50.

"The prevailing mentality," said Tomlin of these moments, "was not so much that we can do it, but more that we have to do it."

Ben found Washington again on the next play for 9 yards, and Moore got the call on second-and-1—the only running play of Ben's Drive—and slithered for 3 yards between the tackles. It was first-and-10 at the Baltimore 38. Ninety seconds remained.

With Ward drawing coverage toward the post, Washington got lonesome on a deep out to Ben's left. Twenty-four yards later, it was first-and-10 at the 14. Seventy-two seconds left. Ben threw quickly to Ward on first down, good for 10 more to the 4. On first and goal, Roethlisberger spiked it.

"I looked to the sideline and said I wanted to clock it," Roethlisberger said. "He [Tomlin] nodded. I just wanted everything to calm down right there."

Probably a mistake. They wasted a down, and wound up saving the Ravens some time on the final possession.

(opposite) Roethlisberger takes the hits and keeps on coming back. Though he is battered, bruised, and beaten up on a weekly basis, he always comes back strong. The hits certainly have not affected his play: he currently sits at seventh all-time in NFL passer rating. (above) Coaches Mike Tomlin and Bill Cowher have shown patience with Roethlisberger during his occasional growing pains. Since becoming the Steelers starter, there have been more highs than lows, and his two Super Bowl rings prove it.

The second-and-goal play was a slightly panicky pass to tight end Matt Spaeth, who didn't get his hands up in time to snare it. Third-and-goal found Ward split wide to the right, the primary receiver.

"I was looking for Hines on a quick curl," Roethlisberger said. "Then Mewelde was the second option. I looked up and it looked like there were about seven guys with Hines and by that time I had to scramble to the left. When I got over there I knew Tone [Holmes] was dragging across to the right, and I started back a little because you know I hold onto the ball too long.

"I was about one half of a second from throwing it away."

Instead he whipped it at Holmes just inside the middle of the end zone, and Holmes caught it at the goal line. Not an inch past it. Not an inch short of it. At the goal line.

Touchdown. Division title. Home playoff game.

"It's a special team," Roethlisberger said.

Yeah. With a special quarterback. ∎

(opposite) Roethlisberger is well known for his charitable work. Whether it is for an ESPN piece or just to make someone's life a little happier, the quarterback is always willing to help out. His work with the Ben Roethlisberger Foundation helps many, not only in Ohio and Pittsburgh, but nationwide as well. (above) With two Super Bowl rings in five seasons, it is not unreasonable to think that Roethlisberger may be heading to Canton if he can stay healthy.

Thrown Together

Roethlisberger has best game of the season as patched-up lineup delivers big road victory

Steelers 26, Jaguars 21 · Sunday, Oct. 5, 2008 · By Ed Bouchette

Ben Roethlisberger and a patched-up Steelers offense lit up Jacksonville, and the fire should glow back in Pittsburgh for a while. Roethlisberger had his best game of the season with 309 yards passing, Mewelde Moore looked like Fast Willie Parker, and the Steelers surprised the Jaguars, 26–21, but not themselves.

"I don't want to use the excuse of people being hurt," linebacker James Harrison said. "We came out here and did what we had to do."

Not everything was new on offense because old-hand Hines Ward caught the winning touchdown pass from Roethlisberger with 1:53 left. Ward, who dropped three earlier passes, including one in the end zone, beat safety Brian Williams to haul in Roethlisberger's 8-yard fade pass in the right corner of the end zone.

"This team showed a lot of character off some adversity," Ward said.

Ward also caught an 18-yard pass four plays earlier on third down with a defender hanging all over Roethlisberger to keep the winning drive going. "Ben held on until the last moment on that in-route," Ward said.

Moore, making his first start for the Steelers because of injuries to Parker and Rashard Mendenhall, ran for 99 yards on 17 carries. The Steelers mixed the run and the pass in a game in which they lost another offensive lineman, tackle Marvel Smith, in the fourth quarter. But the line performed well and Moore, with some help from Gary Russell, made the ground game

go. They rushed for 129 yards and Roethlisberger completed 26 of 41 passes, three for touchdowns.

The victory lifted the Steelers to 4–1 and a big lead in the AFC North Division as they take next weekend off. "Great night for the Steelers," an excited coach Mike Tomlin said. "Guys stepped outside their lanes and delivered."

It was not easy, despite the Steelers late scoring drive and early domination.

The Jaguars came alive in the second half after managing little on offense and scored a go-ahead touchdown on David Garrard's 24-yard pass to tight end Marcedes Lewis early in the fourth quarter. That made it 21–20 and, as the clock wore down in the fourth quarter, it appeared that score might stand and ruin the command the Steelers had shown most of the game.

Using short drops by Roethlisberger, quick passes, deep passes, maximum protection, and an occasional run, the Steelers offense was aggressive early and dominated Jacksonville in the first half. Roethlisberger threw three touchdown passes in the first half—a 1-yarder to Heath Miller, 48 yards to Nate Washington, and the other 72 yards to Jacksonville cornerback Rashean Mathis on an interception.

It was Mathis' third interception return for a touchdown against the Steelers. The Jaguars also scored on Maurice Jones-Drew's 1-yard run in the first quarter. That gave them a 14–7 advantage.

The Steelers came back from that deficit to take a

After rushing for a combined 375 yards in their previous two games, the Jaguars run attack was stymied by the Pittsburgh defense, gaining just 38 yards. The Jaguars were held to 213 total yards.

20–14 halftime lead, but they had to think they wasted chances to go up by much more. They held a whopping 300–50 advantage in yards gained and a 21–4 edge in first downs.

"I didn't feel we were stopped at all in the first half," Roethlisberger said.

The Steelers did not open the game with a pass. Instead they started in a big way on the ground when Moore ran 19 yards on the game's first play. A roughing penalty against Jacksonville tacked on another 15, and the Steelers had a first down at the Jacksonville 49.

Their next four plays were all passes—one incomplete, one a sack for minus-8 yards, and the next a touchdown…for Jacksonville. Santonio Holmes, the intended receiver, fell down as Roethlisberger cut loose and Mathis easily intercepted the pass. He returned it 72 yards for a touchdown, his third interception return for a score against the Steelers and second in his past five games against them.

When the Steelers got the ball after the kickoff, they mixed things up a little more between the run and the pass and gave the ball to three different running backs. Moore carried three times and caught a pass, Gary Russell carried three times, and Najeh Davenport picked up a third-and-1 with a 3-yard run.

Holmes caught a 16-yard pass on third-and-10, and Miller grabbed a 9-yard pass on third down, taking it to the 3. Two plays later the Steelers lined up with four tight ends, including tackle Max Starks, packed into the offense and an I-formation. Roethlisberger faked a hand-off, rolled right, and hit Miller on the 1-yard touchdown pass that tied it, 7–7.

Jacksonville's offense took the field for the first time with 5:12 to go in the first quarter and used two key third-down plays and a penalty to go back on top, 14–7. Receiver Matt Jones was involved in all three. He caught a 15-yard pass on third-and-9, an 18-yard pass

on third-and-10, and then was the victim of a 39-yard Ike Taylor pass interference penalty in the end zone that put the ball at the 1. Maurice Jones-Drew drove up the middle for the 1-yard touchdown run for the Jaguars.

The Steelers scored again on the next drive that ended with Reed's 38-yard field goal early in the second quarter, cutting the Jaguars' lead to 14–10. About that time, the predictions of a low-scoring game were being trashed.

Jacksonville became the first team to punt, in the second quarter, and the Steelers responded with another touchdown. This one came quickly, too, after they started at their 18. Holmes caught the first pass for 19 yards and Washington the second for 14 yards. The fourth play of the drive began from Jacksonville's 48. With an empty set, Roethlisberger took the snap in the shotgun, pump-faked, and Washington sped past flat-footed cornerback Will James. Wide open, Washington caught the ball and stepped freely about 20 yards into the end zone.

Washington finished with 94 yards on six receptions, and Ward had 90 yards on seven catches.

Washington's score gave the Steelers their first lead of the night, 17–14. They extended it to 20–14 at the half when Reed kicked his second field goal, this one from 43 yards, with 45 seconds left. ■

Two of Ben Roethlisberger's biggest completions came with Jaguars defenders in his face on the game-winning drive. Roethlisberger completed both passes and capped the drive with an eight-yard strike to Hines Ward to give the Steelers the win.

Give Me More

Running back Mewelde Moore scores three TDs in dominating performance in the Queen City

Steelers 38, Bengals 10 · Sunday, Oct. 19, 2008 · By Ed Bouchette

October games, December games, playoff games, and meaningless games. Close games, wipeouts, overtimes. There are many ways to skin a cat, and the Steelers have used them all when they've played the Bengals in Paul Brown Stadium.

The Steelers won their eighth in a row in PBS (PittsBurgh Stadium?), something the Bengals have never done. The 38–10 rout came late, but it seemed only a matter of time before the Steelers exerted themselves in this town again.

"Here in a hostile environment against a division opponent on the road—we don't take those for granted," Steelers coach Mike Tomlin said after a late, three-touchdown explosion by his team.

If the Steelers were looking past the winless Bengals (0–7) to the New York Giants, it was only apparent in the second quarter when they hit a lull. The rest of the game, they were dominant.

Halfback Mewelde Moore pulled off the second-best imitation of the weekend after Tina Fey when he filled in for injured Willie Parker and ran like Willie Parker. Moore scored three touchdowns—two rushing and one receiving—and topped 100 yards for the first time in a Steelers uniform. He ran 20 times for 120 yards.

"It's awesome to come here, be the new guy, step in, study hard, work hard, and see your hard work paying off," said Moore.

Ben Roethlisberger, who loves playing the Bengals, completed 17 of 28 passes for 216 yards and two touchdowns, the first one of the game to Moore for 2 yards and his last to Nate Washington of 50 yards. Hines Ward even caught Byron Leftwich's first touchdown pass with the Steelers of 16 yards in the fourth quarter—and Jeff Reed remained perfect on the season when he kicked a 21-yard field goal.

Even better for Roethlisberger, he was not sacked, only the second time that has happened the past two seasons, both against the Bengals. On the other end, the Steelers sacked Cincinnati quarterback Ryan Fitzpatrick seven times with linebackers James Harrison, LaMarr Woodley, and Lawrence Timmons picking up two apiece.

"Even as we were shooting ourselves in the foot a little bit in the first half," Tomlin said, "I thought we were controlling the line of scrimmage."

The Steelers led by just 10–7 at halftime. They moved 75 yards in nine plays to open the game, two of them long passes on third down from Roethlisberger to Ward for 29 yards and to Santonio Holmes for 32 yards. The latter put the ball on the 2 and Roethlisberger deftly faked a handoff to Najeh Davenport, rolled quickly right, and hit Moore wide open in the end zone for a 7–0 lead.

Things looked so easy in the first quarter that the Steelers may have gotten a little greedy. Harrison and Aaron Smith blew up an end-around for a 15-yard loss and then a 15-yard punt gave the Steelers a first down at the Bengals' 30. They moved to a first down at the

Starting for an injured Willie Parker, reserve back Mewelde Moore rushed for 120 yards and two touchdowns and added a third receiving. The 100-yard effort was Moore's first since 2005.

3, but then three consecutive passes fell incomplete and Reed came on to make it 10–0 with a 21-yard field goal near the end of the first quarter.

Cincinnati did not get a first down in its first five series, then strung together seven of them on their sixth possession, ending with Johnson's 5-yard catch for a touchdown. So, while the Steelers dominated the Bengals early, they led by only three points at halftime.

"There was disappointment in the way we played, disappointment the game was that close," safety Ryan Clark said. "Not because of Cincinnati's record or who they were, but because of the opportunities we were giving them in first half."

The Steelers' first drive of the second half produced their second touchdown and a 17–7 lead. Moore scored again, taking a hand-off on third down and, behind an outstanding trap block from guard Darnell Stapleton, ran untouched around left end for 13 yards and the score.

The Bengals responded with a 26-yard field goal by Dave Rayner to make it 17–10 late in the third quarter. Midway through the final period, though, all doubt ended. From the 50, Roethlisberger faked a hand-off and lofted a pass at least 60 yards in the air. Washington had cornerback Geoff Pope, signed Friday from Cincinnati's practice squad, beaten by a step.

"We saw something on the sideline that we thought we could take advantage of," Roethlisberger said. "I used play-action, got the safety to kind of sit there, looked him down, and the next thing I know Nate's just taking off. He's so fast the only thing I could think of was to throw it out there and let him run under it."

Washington caught the ball over his shoulders in the middle of the end zone to make it 24–10.

Timmons sacked Fitzpatrick to end the next Cincinnati series, and on the Steelers' next drive Moore ran 2 yards to make it 31–10. Then Leftwich replaced Roethlisberger and completed the rout with his touchdown toss to Ward.

"There is room for us to improve," Ward said. "We've got a lot of guys banged up, and we have a tough stretch of games ahead of us."

There is relief at the end of that stretch, though, because the Steelers' fourth home game in the next five is against the Bengals. ■

(opposite) Hines Ward saw this pass get broken up by the Bengals' secondary, but he still caught four passes for 60 yards and a score. (above) Ward races into the end zone on his 16-yard, fourth-quarter touchdown. The Byron Leftwich toss was the final score of the 21-point last stanza, providing the final 38–10 margin.

Hines Ward

The ultimate love-hate player

By Ron Cook

Since Hines Ward joined the Steelers in 1998 and began what is looking more and more like a Hall of Fame NFL career, the team has a 113–71–1 record. He is not into ranking wins, but, if he were, surely the one against the Seattle Seahawks in Super Bowl XL, when he was the MVP, would be No. 1. Just as surely, the 14 wins against the Baltimore Ravens would be next.

"There is nothing like beating Baltimore," a very satisfied Ward said as he strolled out of M&T Bank Stadium with a 13–9 smackdown of the Ravens, the AFC North Division title, and a first-round playoff bye.

That's why Ward enjoyed his conversations late in the game with Ravens All-Pros Ray Lewis and Ed Reed so much. "I told 'em both that we were about to score and beat 'em in their own back yard," Ward said, almost giggling.

"No, you ain't!" Lewis and Reed screamed back among a few other unprintable words.

Well, guess what?

Ben Roethlisberger's 4-yard touchdown pass to wide receiver Santonio Holmes with 43 seconds left broke the Ravens' hearts. But what really ticked them off were Ward's contributions to the winning, 12-play, 92-yard drive: three catches for 36 yards.

Losing is one thing in Baltimore. Losing to Ward and the Steelers is something much worse, especially when the defeat could have ended up costing the Ravens a playoff slot.

"I'm pretty sure I'm the most-hated guy down here," Ward said, smiling again.

Smirking, actually.

"I love being the most-hated guy here," he said. "I love beating them while [their fans] are flicking me off."

It goes back to a 2001 game when Ward drilled Ravens safety Rod Woodson with a block and bloodied his nose, prompting Woodson to swear he would get even. Last season, Ward popped Reed and linebacker Bart Scott with brutal blocks, leading Scott to promise to "kill" Ward. Earlier this season, linebacker Terrell Suggs went on a national radio show and said the Ravens had a bounty on Ward when the teams played September 29.

"I know Hines is loving this," Steelers linebacker James Farrior said after Ward's eight-catch, 107-yard game. "He always has a chip on his shoulder when he plays these guys because he knows they're going to come at him and try to do something bad to him."

For a long time, it looked as if the Ravens would inflict the worst kind of pain on Ward—a Steelers loss. They led 9–3 going into the fourth quarter and he had done very little. He had two short catches on the Steelers' first possession, then had just one on their next nine, although that 21-yard play set up their second-quarter field goal.

But Ward had five catches for 74 yards in the fourth quarter, all five for first downs. His 30-yard reception set up the field goal that pulled the Steelers to 9–6. Then, he

The contagious smile of Hines Ward is known to football fans around the world. A noted philanthropist, Ward is a giving personality and one of the most charitable players in the National Football League.

had those three catches on the deciding drive.

"I'm not surprised by anything that Hines Ward does," Farrior said. "He's the ultimate competitor."

Said Ward, "I thrive on wanting the ball in the fourth quarter. Some guys don't want it. They shy away from it in the big situations. I want it. I love it."

Holmes and wide receiver Nate Washington have had some big moments this season, but they aren't nearly as consistent as Ward. If I'm Roethlisberger, I'm looking for Ward or tight end Heath Miller in every critical spot. It seems amazing now that the Steelers were able to beat the Dallas Cowboys December 7 with Ward getting just one catch for 2 yards. He also had only one catch two weeks earlier against the Cincinnati Bengals.

"It's hard and it gets frustrating, but we're winning," Ward said. "It's a lot easier to get over it when we're winning. I like getting the ball, just like all receivers do. But you'll never hear me being a T.O."– Terrell Owens of the Dallas Cowboys–"because that's not my style. I just try to make plays when my number is called. I don't make all of them, but my percentage is pretty good."

Especially against the Ravens. Excluding his rookie season, Ward has 95 catches for 1,167 yards and six touchdowns in 20 games against Baltimore. This was the sixth time he had at least eight catches against the Ravens.

If Ward had a regret, it's that he wasn't able to finish a block on Scott late in the third quarter. He peeled back on a Roethlisberger scramble and had Scott lined up for a legal hit only to go over top of him when Scott ducked.

"They put a bounty on me and then he ducks," Ward said, shrugging.

"He saw Hines coming and he was scared!" Holmes crowed from two lockers down.

It didn't matter in the end. Ward didn't need to knock Scott into next week to go home feeling happy. The win was plenty good enough. ∎

(opposite) Known for his impressive postseason performances, the pressure of the playoffs seems to elevate Ward's game to another level. Seen here in action during the AFC Championship Game, Ward was named the MVP of Super Bowl XL. (above) Ward has some of the most reliable hands in football. He had four straight 1,000-yard seasons between 2001 and 2004 and reached the mark again in 2008.

Snapped Out of It

Roethlisberger throws four picks; errant snap lifts Super Bowl champs to win at Heinz Field

Giants 21, Steelers 14 • Sunday, Oct. 26, 2008 • By Ed Bouchette

Their march through the NFC East Division proved a costly one for the Steelers. In Philadelphia, they lost Willie Parker, Casey Hampton, and the game. Against the New York Giants at Heinz Field, they lost long-snapper Greg Warren and their second game in seven.

"That's a championship-caliber football team," Steelers coach Mike Tomlin said after the reigning Super Bowl champs came from behind to beat the Steelers, 21–14. "It doesn't go down easy. It's tough to swallow."

Tough because the Steelers led, 14–9, midway through the fourth quarter when the Giants scored three times to snatch the game away from them. Tough because their passing game was a wreck—Ben Roethlisberger threw four interceptions, was sacked five times, and completed 13 of 29 passes. Tough, because they wasted another good game from their defense.

"It's disappointing, offensively, top to bottom and it starts with me," Roethlisberger said. "I felt we left the defense down."

The Steelers defense—although it produced no sacks and no turnovers—held the Giants (6–1) to four John Carney field goals until tight end Kevin Boss caught Eli Manning's 2-yard pass for New York's only touchdown, the winner, with 3:07 to go. That was set up in the third quarter when Warren left for the season with a torn ACL. The Steelers had no true backup long-snapper, but linebacker James Harrison volunteered after fooling around with snapping the past few training camps.

He never snapped in a game, not even high school. He was called to snap from the Steelers' 17 and his team leading, 14–12. Nerves and adrenaline took hold and he snapped it high over punter Mitch Berger's head and over the end line for a 2-point safety that tied it.

The Giants took over at their 47 and moved in for the kill when Manning (19 of 32 for 199 yards) completed a 25-yard, third-down pass to Steve Smith to the 25. Three plays later, Bass scored the winner.

"They proved why they are champs," Steelers receiver Hines Ward said. "They came into our back yard and beat us at home."

The Steelers made their plays in the first three quarters. Mewelde Moore scored on another long run, from 32 yards, on the first series. Nate Washington caught his third long touchdown pass in the past three games, a 65-yarder to put the Steelers in front 14–9. He caught another one later but a holding penalty erased it.

Moore finished with 84 yards in his third consecutive start, but was not as effective in the second half, when he had just 21 of those yards. "There is only one stat that matters to us," Tomlin said when asked about Moore's game, "and that is winning. We didn't do it today."

Carney kicked his first field goal for a 7–3 score, then James Butler intercepted Roethlisberger, who had 189 yards passing. The Giants drove to a first down at the Steelers' 2 after the turnover, when things got interesting. They had a second down at the 1 and Brandon Jacobs carried for no gain, then scored. But Tomlin

Mewelde Moore had his second straight strong game in the place of Willie Parker. He tore off a 30-yard touchdown run in the first quarter and finished with 84 yards on 19 carries.

Mike Tomlin

Coach's early career looking an awful lot like Cowher's

By Gerry Dulac

Nobody is really sure which player was the first to be "posted" by the new coach—Larry Foote or Hines Ward. Not that it really mattered. What mattered was that one of the two veterans stepped afoul of the guidelines set forth by Mike Tomlin and found their names posted in the locker room on something called "The News."

In Foote's case, he had reported to minicamp a couple pounds heavier than the previous season. "It could be good news or it could be bad news, but, normally, it's bad news," Foote said. "If you see 'The News' on that board the whole locker room goes, 'Oh-oh, someone's in trouble.'"

That's how it started with Mike Tomlin. That's how he began to change the climate with the Steelers, how he started to get the attention of his players, how he started to convince them there will be a standard to which they will all be held.

"You do something outside the realm of his authority, he'd post it out there," Ward said. "He wouldn't do anything about it. But he was putting you out there. He would let your teammates judge you."

Little by little, Tomlin held them accountable. Foote. Ward. All of them. Didn't matter if they were Pro Bowl veterans or rookie free agents. He treated them all the same, demanded the same. And, little by little, he broke them down, too. Changed the way they practiced. Changed what they could wear to practice. Took what they had done under Bill Cowher—a way

that was immensely successful—and changed that, too, never mind that the Steelers were just two years removed from a Super Bowl championship when Tomlin arrived.

"Coming in behind a legendary coach in Bill Cowher, how he handled himself, has been tremendous," said defensive end Nick Eason. "It wasn't an easy task."

But Tomlin did it. He didn't change the defense, even though the concepts under which he learned—a 4-3 alignment, Cover-two in the secondary, little blitzing—were philosophically different from the scheme and style employed by defensive coordinator Dick LeBeau. He didn't try to change the offense that was being implemented by Bruce Arians, who spent the previous three seasons as a wide receiver coach in an offense run by Ken Whisenhunt, Tomlin's coaching counterpart on the field in Super Bowl XLIII.

Rather, he was more interested in changing the way the players believe. And what they believe. More specifically, he wanted to get them to believe in him. Get them to believe in what he does.

"There really wasn't resentment, but it was a little uncertainty," said Ward, an 11-year veteran with the most continuous years of service on the roster. "We just came off two years since we won a Super Bowl and he came down on us—you had to wear long shells to practice, you had to wear full gear, guys couldn't go out there with Georgia shirts or their alumni schools underneath their uniforms. He wanted it to be team-issued stuff.

Head coach Mike Tomlin has enjoyed nothing but success in Pittsburgh, winning division titles in each of his first two years. Including the playoffs, he is now 25–11 as a head coach.

"It could have been like, 'Man, why is this guy doing all this stuff? We just won a Super Bowl. Who's to say you can come in and change it?' But there was none of that. It was like, OK, this is what you want? Whatever. We'll test it and see how far we can go."

Two years later, they have discovered how far they can go: all the way to a Super Bowl, becoming the first franchise to win six Super Bowl titles.

Impressive?

That's the word Art Rooney II, the Steelers president, used to describe Tomlin the first time he met him. It was the defining word then. And it's the applicable word now.

There is little about Tomlin that is not impressive. That was apparent immediately to Tampa Bay Buccaneers defensive coordinator Monte Kiffin the first time he met Tomlin in 2001. Tomlin, an assistant at the University of Cincinnati, was interviewing to become the Buccaneers' secondary coach.

"You could feel the room come alive," Kiffin said.

Indeed, Tomlin is no ordinary NFL coach. He reads and quotes Robert Frost, uses expressions such as "thoughtfully non-rhythmic," "standard of expectation," and "iron sharpens iron," and is never unprepared for any question. His weekly Tuesday news conference, a feeder system for YouTube, could become a training film for orators and debaters, right down to the expressionless faces he often uses to accompany his delivery.

"The sharpness, his quickness on his feet, there is no panic in him," said former Detroit Lions Coach Rod Marinelli, an assistant coach with Tomlin at Tampa Bay. "When you're confident in yourself and your abilities, you can go a long way."

Not a surprise for a person who attended William & Mary, a school that produces presidents and, as Tomlin once noted, "No dummies."

(opposite) A renowned teacher of the game, Tomlin knows when to comfort and when to ride his players, a skill that cannot be taught. (above) After starting his coaching career at the Virginia Military Institute, Tomlin had never been a head coach until the Steelers hired him away from the Minnesota Vikings.

"You never can stump the guy," said inside line-backer James Farrior, who is just three years younger than Tomlin and even played against him in college when Tomlin was at the University of Virginia. "He's got an answer for everything, no matter what it is. "

"It's hard to question him because he is so intelligent," said defensive end Aaron Smith. "He doesn't do anything just to do it. He always has a reason or a thought process. I think sometimes you'll get intimidated because he's not going to be a politician. He's not going to be rude or abrasive, but he's not going to be a guy who will do what everyone else thinks we should do."

It has not been as easy task. A shoulder separation sustained by his $100 million quarterback in the season opener. A knee injury to his Pro Bowl running back in Week 4. Four new starters on an offensive line that has been adequate at best, disorganized and ineffective at worst. Three different punters. A secondary in which one cornerback had a broken forearm and a safety had two dislocated shoulders. And the league's toughest schedule.

And look what happened: The second-best record in the NFL. One of only two teams—Arizona is the other—to be undefeated in the division. An AFC Championship Game victory at Heinz Field…finally. A sixth Super Bowl title, more than any other franchise.

"I am always going to be open to change, if it produces better results," Tomlin said a few days before the game. "Like every year I have been in this profession, I analyze the things I have done and how I potentially could have done something better to produce a better outcome. My intentions were to do that last year. Thankfully, we are where we sit here today. I don't know if it is any way directly related to some of the decisions that I made, but I will always be searching for the ceiling in terms of putting our team in the best position to perform."

He might have to search higher. In two years, the ceiling has already been raised to impressive heights. ∎

(opposite) Tomlin has ably picked up where the Steelers' inimitable coaching legacy left off and has kept them atop the AFC. (above) Even when he watches a field goal sail through the uprights, Tomlin's intensity is apparent.

Capital D

Steelers fight through pain, top Redskins

Steelers 23, Redskins 6 • Monday, Nov. 3, 2008 • By Ed Bouchette

The Steelers won't say they thrive off their injuries, but they did it again—and this was the big one.

It was all about shoulders. Quarterback Ben Roethlisberger left the game at halftime with a right shoulder injury. Byron Leftwich replaced him and carried the Steelers on his shoulders to a 23–6 victory against the Washington Redskins.

"I can play this game," said Leftwich, a Washington D.C., native who described himself as a "die-hard Redskins fan." "I can play this game in Canada, I can play this game in Alaska, I can play this game anywhere."

Their first win against an NFC East team in three tries this year lifted the Steelers to 6–2 at the midway point of the season.

Roethlisberger said his right shoulder was injured when he pulled a quarterback sneak for a 1-yard touchdown with 32 seconds left in the first half. Earlier in the second quarter, he shook his right hand in pain after it struck a defensive player on a follow through. Roethlisberger completed just 5 of 17 passes for 50 yards and one interception. He said after the game that he felt he would be "OK."

Leftwich came on, and the Steelers' sluggish offense came to life. He led them to a touchdown on his first drive after completing a 50-yard pass to Nate Washington. Willie Parker, who finished with 70 yards rushing in his first game since September 21, ended that drive with a 1-yard touchdown run. Leftwich then

guided them to a second touchdown early in the fourth quarter, throwing a 5-yard pass to Santonio Holmes to complete a 12-play, 77-yard scoring drive.

Leftwich, signed as a free agent in August after Charlie Batch's collarbone was broken, completed 7 of 10 passes for 129 yards and one touchdown. "Byron Leftwich came home tonight to D.C. and put together a winning performance for us," Coach Mike Tomlin said. "He's a popular guy in that locker room right now."

Leftwich had help on the other side of the ball, too, because the Steelers' defense suffocated the Redskins. They sacked Washington quarterback Jason Campbell seven times with LaMarr Woodley getting two and James Harrison one and a half. They held the Redskins to 60 yards rushing and 221 total yards.

When Washington had a good drive going in Steelers territory late in the third quarter, cornerback Deshea Townsend stopped it with an interception at the 23, the first interception thrown by Jason Campbell this season, ending a Redskins record of 271 completions without one.

"That was big," Townsend acknowledged. "It was one of the best drives they had going. The one thing about the West Coast offense, once you get a bead on it, you can figure it out. We stopped the run, we got to the quarterback well, and we didn't give up big plays and, when you do that, chances are you're going to win."

The defense kept the Steelers in the game early while the offense did little and a roll of the dice put them in a quick hole. Tomlin's gamble on the opening

Washington native Byron Leftwich got a rude homecoming from the Redskins defense on this play, but the Steelers' backup had a day to remember. He completed 7 of 10 passes for 129 yards and a touchdown, leading the offense to two scores that put the game away.

kickoff backfired when the Redskins recovered an onside attempt, and turned it into a 3–0 lead on Shaun Suisham's 44-yard field goal.

"We came in to play aggressively," Tomlin explained.

The Redskins then intercepted Roethlisberger's third pass on the Steelers' first series. Defensive end Andre Carter batted the pass into the air, and it bounced off the back of offensive tackle Max Starks and into the hands of defensive tackle Cornelius Griffin at the Steelers' 30. Again, the Redskins could not pick up a first down, so Suisham booted a 43-yard field goal for a 6–0 lead.

The Steelers finally scored with 8:09 left in the first half on Jeff Reed's 35-yard field goal.

The Steelers took their first lead in rare fashion—set up by a blocked punt.

A sack and a penalty pushed the Steelers back to the 24, but Roethlisberger completed a 9-yard pass to Holmes and, on third down, 12 yards to Ward. Roethlisberger finished the drive by sneaking less than a yard to the left of center Justin Hartwig. Soon after, the seemingly indestructible quarterback was running

into the locker room to be checked by the doctors.

Leftwich added some quick punch when he replaced Roethlisberger to start the second half. His first pass was caught by Nate Washington for a 50-yard completion. Leftwich then completed a key third-down pass of 7 yards to Mewelde Moore to the 1, and Parker scored from there. Reed missed the extra point, hooking it wide left to keep the Steelers' lead at 16–6. It was Reed's first such miss since 2003.

After Townsend's interception ended a Redskins drive, Leftwich took the Steelers back on another scoring ride. He completed passes of 16 to Holmes, 13 and 25 to Mewelde Moore, and 13 on third down to Ward. He then rifled a pass in the left front corner to Holmes, who dived over the pylon for a touchdown. Reed banged home the point this time, and the Steelers led 23–6 early in the fourth quarter.

"I wasn't going to be denied, man," Holmes said.

Tomlin challenged a ruling that Campbell scored from 6 yards out with 7:19 left, and replays clearly showed that both Campbell's knee and shoulder touched the ground a yard before the goal line. ∎

(opposite) Ben Roethlisberger scored on a plunge to give the Steelers the lead, but it was his last play of the game. He aggravated his shoulder injury and was forced to watch the rest of the game from the sideline. (above) Willie Parker made his return to action from injury, rushing for 70 yards on 21 carries, capped by a third quarter touchdown.

Dropping the Ball

AFC North lead melts away as Big Ben throws three interceptions, Steelers muff two potential picks

Colts 24, Steelers 20 • Sunday, Nov. 9, 2008 • By Ed Bouchette

Everything, it seemed, slipped through the Steelers' hands: two interceptions dropped by Ike Taylor and Troy Polamalu, a 10-point lead they held on the Indianapolis Colts, and their first-place cushion in the AFC North. What once looked to be a commanding lead in their division slipped away to nothing when the Steelers lost their second consecutive game at Heinz Field, 24–20, to the Colts in a fashion new to them.

It had been 40 years since the Colts last won in Pittsburgh, and it may be another 40 before the Steelers forget how that drought ended.

Ben Roethlisberger (30 of 42, 284 yards) threw three interceptions and no touchdowns, and Taylor and Polamalu dropped potential interceptions that made a 14-point difference, and the Steelers could not run on the 25th-ranked run defense in the NFL.

"We didn't do the things that we normally do to win games," linebacker James Harrison said. "We had the lead at the end and let it slip away."

They also suddenly cannot run the ball. The Steelers managed only 55 net yards, 57 of them from starter Mewelde Moore on 24 carries. While Moore scored on two short touchdown runs, he and his teammates could not punch it in from the 2 in a crucial fourth-quarter attempt. Moore was stopped twice by defensive tackle Eric Foster, and Jeff Reed kicked a short field goal to put the Steelers in front, 20–17, yet knowing they had blown a chance to go up by a touchdown.

Peyton Manning and the Colts (5–4) made them

pay five minutes later. After cornerback Tim Jennings pilfered a Roethlisberger pass at the Steelers' 32, it took Indianapolis only four plays to take its only lead. Manning found running back Dominic Rhodes behind a scrambling Polamalu and threw a 17-yard touchdown pass to him with 3:04 left. It was Manning's third touchdown pass of the game, and it stood as the winner when Roethlisberger's Hail Mary pass from the 27 into the Colts' end zone was intercepted on the last play.

"That was my man," inside linebacker James Farrior admitted of the Colts' winning touchdown. "I had him man-to-man, they ran a fake toss to him. I thought it was a running play. He slipped out of the backfield, and I kind of sorta lost track of him. That wasn't Troy's fault."

Polamalu's error occurred earlier, near the end of the first half with the Steelers ahead 17–7. Manning, who was not having a particularly good day (21 of 40, 240 yards), threw a pass right to Polamalu near the Steelers' 30. With 70 yards of green Heinz Field grass and nothing else in front of him, he dropped it. Three plays later, cornerback Keiwan Ratliff, taken off the scrap heap earlier this year by the Colts, intercepted Roethlisberger with 1:24 left. Manning turned that one into gold, too, by throwing a 2-yard touchdown pass to tight end Dallas Clark with six seconds left. It was game on at halftime, 17–14.

"If this were an individual sport and I lost the game, I wouldn't feel so bad," Roethlisberger said. "It's letting

---

In a game decided by inches, the difference between a touchdown and incompletion can come down to fingertips. Ike Taylor got a piece of this pass, but Reggie Wayne was able to haul it in for a touchdown that tied the game in the first quarter.

the guys down, letting your teammates down. It hurts. You never hear me say 'I' anything, but I lost this game."

He rarely threw deep, although that was due more to the Cover-2 umbrella defense the Colts played than a sore shoulder. If Roethlisberger's arm was sore, he did nothing to let on while completing all four of his passes for 48 yards on the opening drive. He threw a 23-yarder to Santonio Holmes and a 16-yarder to Nate Washington before Moore scored from 1 yard.

The Colts struck quickly to tie it 7–7. The Steelers used an old-fashioned flea-flicker to reclaim the lead, 14–7, early in the second quarter. From the Colts' 42, Roethlisberger handed off to Moore, who took a step forward, stopped, and flipped the ball back to his quarterback. The pitch was a little high, but Roethlisberger pulled it down and threw a pass to Ward deep on the right. Ward eluded safety Bob Sanders to catch it at the 10, circled around, and ran it to the 1. Moore scored standing up on the next play.

Jeff Reed put the Steelers ahead, 17–7, when he kicked a 42-yard field goal with 4:18 left in the half, and that's when things started breaking the other way. First came Polamalu's drop, then Ratliff's interception and Clark's touchdown before the half.

Indianapolis tied it 17–17 on the first drive of the second half, moving 56 yards in a dozen plays and ending it with Adam Vinatieri's 36-yard field goal.

Reed put the Steelers back on top with his 24-yard field goal, but they weren't celebrating. "That's typical Steelers, and we didn't come through," Ward said. "It was a huge turnaround. You put up seven points, and it puts more pressure on them. They shut us down, and we end up kicking a field goal."

And, later, kicking themselves.

"We felt like we had this game and we lost it," Ward said. ∎

(opposite) Tight end Matt Spaeth had his best game of the season, catching six passes for 53 yards. (above) Hines Ward made eight catches in this hard-hitting game, racking up 112 yards without scoring.

A Point Made

Fourth-quarter drive sets up winning FG in final seconds by Jeff Reed

Steelers 11, Chargers 10 · Sunday, Nov. 16, 2008 · By Ed Bouchette

Mike Tomlin vowed he did not have quarterback Ben Roethlisberger on a pitch count, and there was no movement in the bullpen as the bend-but-don't-score Steelers offense lined up for one final time at its 13, trailing San Diego by two points. Defensive end Aaron Smith said he had "all the confidence in the world" that the offense could pull it out, even though it had given him no reason to believe that it would.

But pull it out the Steelers did. On a cold, snowy day in which they moved up and down the field almost like no other this season, but never officially reached the end zone, the Steelers' offense mounted a 13-play, 73-yard drive that covered 6 minutes, 30 seconds. Jeff Reed ended it by kicking his third field goal, from 32 yards with 11 seconds left, and the Steelers managed an 11–10 victory against the San Diego Chargers. It was the first time an NFL game was decided by that score.

"I think that was important for us to do that," Smith said of the final drive. "We've been in close games that we haven't won."

They also had not won at home in their previous two at Heinz Field, they did not score a touchdown, and they barely beat a team with a losing record. But that final drive could mean everything to the Steelers by the end of the regular season.

"It was a great team victory for us," said Tomlin.

While Roethlisberger did not throw a touchdown pass and was sacked four times, he completed 31 of 41 passes for 308 yards. "We were taking what they were

giving us and playing pitch-and-catch," Tomlin said.

Roethlisberger's performance, Willie Parker's notable return to play with 115 yards rushing, and Hines Ward's 124 yards on 11 receptions—410 yards of total—are statistics that would normally equate to more than 11 points. But the Steelers lost 115 yards on 13 penalties compared to just 5 yards on two penalties for the Chargers. They even had two touchdowns called back by penalties—one of their own, and another on an admitted mistake by the officials. Parker had a 4-yard touchdown run cancelled by a holding penalty and that led to Reed's winning kick on the next play.

And Troy Polamalu's 12-yard return of a fumble on the last play of the game was overruled—wrongly, referee Scott Green admitted afterward—because of an illegal forward pass by San Diego as it tried desperately to keep a play going with laterals. Nevertheless, the Steelers had won and their defense again was the impetus.

"They have been really good for us all year," Roethlisberger said.

Reed, who had his first miss of the season early, kicked his eighth winning field goal and second this season. Linebacker James Harrison was the only other Steelers player to score when he stripped the ball from Rivers in the end zone for a safety that ultimately proved to be the difference.

LaDainian Tomlinson did score the game's only touchdown from 3 yards out in the first quarter, but

Willie Parker had a strong game in his return after missing the contest against the Colts. He finished without a touchdown, but racked up 115 yards on 25 carries.

he was held to 57 yards and the Chargers to just 66 yards rushing.

San Diego's opening score came after the Steelers failed to take advantage of an acrobatic, one-handed interception by Polamalu. Ike Taylor hit Chargers receiver Vince Jackson as he was bobbling a potential reception and the ball popped up. Polamalu raced over, dived and got his right hand under the ball before it could hit the ground, and made the interception. But Reed was wide left from 51 yards, and the Steelers blew another scoring opportunity.

The Steelers cracked the scoreboard twice in the second quarter and Harrison was in the middle of both. He stripped Rivers of the ball in the end zone, the Chargers recovered and the Steelers had a safety. The Steelers trailed, 7–2, but they were on the board.

"That was huge, a big momentum swing," Smith said. Then, with San Diego driving toward a possible

bigger lead at the Steelers' 17 just before the half, Harrison intercepted Rivers and returned it 33 yards to the Steelers' 43. That led to Reed's 21-yard field goal with no time left and a 7–5 San Diego halftime lead.

"James Harrison continues to make splash play after splash play for us," Tomlin said of his Pro Bowl linebacker who recorded his 12th sack of the season on the safety.

But for how well they played all day, the Steelers' defense allowed a 17-play, 78-yard drive by San Diego that ended with Kaeding kicking a 22-yard field goal with 6:41 to go. Still, they did not let the Chargers into the end zone.

"The last two games we lost at home in close games," safety Ryan Clark said. "A lot of talk has been about finishing. For our offense to go down, drive the ball, score a touchdown, have that called back, come in and kick a field goal is a huge play for us and a huge drive." ■

(opposite) Backup Gary Russell plunges ahead on one of his two carries. The ground game finished with 124 yards total. (above) Hines Ward had a game-high 11 receptions for 124 yards, accounting for more than one-third of Ben Roethlisberger's 308 yards through the air.

Keeping Warm

Roethlisberger, Steelers overcome wintry conditions again to solidify AFC North lead

Steelers 27, Bengals 10 • Thursday, Nov. 20, 2008 • By Ed Bouchette

The Steelers and Cincinnati played as if they had little rest between games, and then the Bengals did what the Bengals do: They went to sleep.

It was cold, windy and snowy at Heinz Field, where the sloppy play of both teams added to the mix before the Steelers prevailed, 27–10. The victory nevertheless boosted the Steelers' record to 8–3 in first place in the AFC North Division while the Bengals stumbled to 1–9–1, the worst record in the conference.

"Being 8–3 in the next few days is nice," said defensive end Aaron Smith, who came through with three batted passes and another dominating performance.

The Steelers, who trailed 7–0 after one period of lackluster play, scored 20 consecutive points on a 3-yard touchdown pass from Ben Roethlisberger to Heath Miller, two Jeff Reed field goals of 37 and 38 yards, and a 2-yard run by Gary Russell. Roethlisberger added another touchdown on an 8-yard scramble late in the game.

"I think we stumbled out of the gate a little bit, both offensively and defensively," coach Mike Tomlin said.

The Bengals scored first on Ryan Fitzpatrick's 10-yard pass to Glenn Holt and late in the fourth quarter on a 26-yard field goal by Shayne Graham.

Tomlin calls it a game of attrition. Not only did the Steelers wear down the Bengals, but some players on both sides also wore out. The most serious might be defensive end Brett Keisel, who left the game in the fourth quarter with a sprained right knee. The Steelers also lost receiver Santonio Holmes and halfback Willie Parker to injuries in the second half.

Roethlisberger had an efficient game, completing 17 of 30 for 243 yards, no interceptions, and no sacks for only the second time this season, the other against the Bengals as well. He also ran three times for 13 yards, picking up a first down on one and a touchdown on the other. Holmes caught five passes for 84 yards.

"It was a blizzard out there," Roethlisberger said of the weather. "I was throwing a lot of sliders out there."

The Steelers scored on three short touchdowns, an area where they've had difficulty this season. "It just felt good to score," said Roethlisberger, who threw his only touchdown pass in the past four games. "We went through that midseason struggle offensively," Roethlisberger said. "I feel like we're going in the right direction."

They were going in no direction early, especially on the ground. Parker's last run of 15 yards gave him 37 total on 14 carries. Mewelde Moore picked things up with 56 yards on 15 carries, and he also caught four passes for 41, including a 22-yard pickup on the rare screen pass.

"Mo has been doing it week in and week out," Roethlisberger said.

Holt replaced Chad Johnson, deactivated and sent home by Bengals coach Marvin Lewis yesterday morning, and he staked his team to a 7–0 lead by catching the 10-yard touchdown pass from Fitzpatrick.

The Steelers tied it 7–7 with 10:16 left in the second quarter on Roethlisberger's 3-yard pass to Miller,

Willie Parker tried to gut it out against the Bengals, but a knee injury forced him to the sideline. He managed 14 carries for 37 yards before leaving the game, and backup Gary Russell scored his first NFL touchdown in Parker's place.

only his second touchdown pass in the past five games. A pass to Hines Ward that covered 37 yards to the 13 made that drive come alive.

Two long passes to Holmes set up the Steelers' second score, Reed's 37-yard field goal, and a 10–7 lead late in the first half. Holmes caught passes of 27 and 22 yards on that 72-yard drive, the second on third-and-9.

The Bengals opened the game without starting defensive end Antwan Odom, who was injured. They lost his replacement, Frostee Rucker, in the first quarter and their other end and leading sacker, Robert Geathers, in the second quarter.

It should have been like shooting ducks in a pond for the Steelers, but they struggled mightily on offense in the first half. Still, they led 10–7 and were driving toward another score in the third quarter. Holmes caught a 19-yard pass on third down to keep the series alive, but his next catch was his last. He caught a 6-yarder over the middle, where he was hit quickly and hard to the head. Holmes was removed from the game with a concussion.

Ward proceeded to drop the next pass, and the Steelers had to settle for Reed's second field goal, from 38 yards, for a 13–7 lead midway through the third quarter. They made it 20 consecutive points when Russell ended a drive with his first NFL touchdown, a 2-yard run around right end.

Lewis made a strange decision when, trailing by 13 points, he opted for a 26-yard Graham field goal on fourth down at the Steelers' 8. That brought Cincinnati within 10 points with 6:47 to go.

The Steelers then drove 73 yards on 11 plays, a drive that ended when Roethlisberger scrambled up the middle on third down for an 8-yard touchdown with 2:15 left.

Troy Polamalu intercepted his fifth pass of the season at the 2 to put an end to it. ■

(opposite) With the winds swirling and wind chills hovering around 20 degrees, both punters had tough games.
(above) Rising from the turf, Ben Roethlisberger awaits the celebration with his teammates after his eight-yard run capped the scoring. Roethlisberger also threw one touchdown pass.

Steelers Defense

Sparkling from any angle

By Gerry Dulac

In the two years he worked as a wide receivers coach with the Steelers, Bob Bratkowski learned one very important lesson about their defense: Man, can they run to the ball. Now, having spent the past eight years trying to solve their defense as the offensive coordinator for the Cincinnati Bengals, Bratkowski discovered another indelible element of their defense: Man, are they good.

And it doesn't seem to matter which aspect of the defense he might seek to attack. Finding a weakness is like trying to find Jimmy Hoffa.

"They get to spots where they are extremely hard to cut off," Bratkowski said. "They're always staying ahead of you. Every year, we look back at all their games, who ran best against them, and we still have a tough time figuring it out. Dick LeBeau has them put together extremely well right now."

The Steelers brought more than the league's top-ranked defense into the postseason when they played the San Diego Chargers at Heinz Field in an AFC divisional playoff game. They trotted out a defense that, statistically, conceptually, and strategically, is one of the best in modern history, a unit perhaps even more complete than the 2000 Baltimore Ravens and one that came within a whisker of several NFL standards.

Consider:

Some teams load up to stop the run and, in the process, sacrifice the pass. Other teams drop extra players into coverage, use a Cover-2 or even Cover-3 scheme to stop the pass, and, in the process, sacrifice the run.

Not the Steelers. They shut down each with equal tenacity. If that's not enough, they also pressure the passer, forcing quarterbacks to run for cover from the AFC's No. 1 sack tandem—outside linebackers LaMarr Woodley and James Harrison, the NFL's Defensive Most Valuable Player.

"They have developed a sense of pride," said Bratkowski, who was with the Steelers in 1999–2000. "You have a lot of teams who have more individual interests in mind but, when you get it like the Steelers get it, when you got 11 guys gang-tackling and running to the ball, that's what's special about them. They play for each other."

The Steelers finished the regular season ranked No. 1 in the league in fewest points (223), total defense (237.2), pass defense (156.9), and yards per play (3.89). They were No. 2 in rush defense (80.3) and sacks (51).

They are a combination of The Steel Curtain and Blitzburgh, a unit that doesn't have a fancy nickname—Woodley suggested The Steel Pit—but certainly one that doesn't need any introduction. They use aggression, speed, and the element of disguise to prevent 100-yard rushers and make many of the league's top-rated passers look like Sunday morning pickup quarterbacks.

"Their consistency, week in and week out, speaks for itself," said LeBeau, the team's defensive coordinator and mastermind of a unit that didn't allow a 100-

A two-time Pro Bowler and the newest NFL Defensive Player of the Year, James Harrison is the rock of the Steelers defense. After spending his first few seasons under the radar, he has exploded into one of the most dominating players in the game.

yard rusher or 300-yard passer this season. "That's definitely the thing I'm most proud of. They just didn't have that low spot, they didn't have that game where the opponent made four or five [big] plays. And, in the NFL, you can play pretty well sometimes and give up three or four pretty good size plays. It's hard to do what they've done."

Talk about domination.... How dominant were the Steelers?

They came within 54 rushing yards of becoming the first team since the 1991 Philadelphia Eagles to lead the NFL in total defense, rush defense, and pass defense. After allowing Cleveland's Jamal Lewis more rushing yards (94) in the regular-season finale than any opposing back this season, they finished second behind the Minnesota Vikings in rush defense, allowing an average of 80.3 yards per game

Another NFL standard also eluded their grasp, though, by a much smaller margin. The Steelers finished the regular season allowing an average of 3.897 yards per play, just 7/1000th of a yard from tying the 16-game record set by the 1979 Tampa Bay Buccaneers, who allowed an average of 3.890 yards per play.

"They look like some of the Steelers defenses in the past, and also they look a lot like Baltimore when they killed everybody and won the Super Bowl that year," said Dallas Cowboys coach Wade Phillips,

whose father, Bum, coached the Houston Oilers teams of the 1970s that faced the great Steel Curtain defense. "They're a stifling defense, and they've played against some good offensive teams and made them look bad. They're playing really well."

The Baltimore defense to which Phillips referred was in 2000 when the Ravens allowed only 165 points, an NFL record for a 16-game season, and won the Super Bowl by allowing just 23 points in four postseason games.

But, while the Ravens' defense led the NFL in points allowed and yards rushing (60.6 yards per game), the unit did not exhibit the same type of total dominance as the Steelers. For example, the Ravens ranked eighth in the league in yards passing (187.3) and just 22nd in sacks (35).

"They have such a great combination of strength and speed," said Tennessee Titans coach Jeff Fisher, whose team was the only one to score more than 24 points against the Steelers this season.

"They close so quickly. I looked back over the course of six to eight games and looked for explosive plays...there are very few of them. When you do find them, the ball carrier is going down right at 20 or 21 yards. They just recover so well because of their team speed."

The Steelers allowed fewer big plays (20 yards or longer) than any team in the league. They ranked No. 1

Troy Polamalu turns up field after intercepting a pass intended for New England Patriots tight end Benjamin Watson in Foxborough, Massachusetts, in November 2008. (above) In addition to being a ferocious hitter, Polamalu can also demonstrate a receiver's touch when the situation calls for it.

in 20-yard runs (4), 20-yard passes (23), and 40-yard passes (2), and tied for second in fewest 40-yard runs (1).

Perhaps the primary reason is the emphasis LeBeau, who has been the team's defensive coordinator since 2004, places on preventing big plays. It is the No. 1 mantra for his players. But right behind that is the importance he places on tackling the ball, or, as he said, forcing the opponent to snap the ball again.

"All I ever sensed from having coached there is that team tackling is like a snowball going downhill— once you get it going, nobody wants to be left out," said Bratkowski. "If somebody isn't pulling their weight, they probably get heat from the other players.

"When I was at the University of Miami, when we won the national championship two out of three years, there was such a pride that a player was afraid to be the guy to make a mistake. Not only did he not want to let his teammates down, he didn't want to let past teammates down. The Steelers are the only other team I've seen like that."

"That's like our trademark," said defensive end Aaron Smith. "When we turn on the film, we want to see a group of guys running to the ball."

Following their leader, the Steelers want to do more than just support each other. They also want to make sure they don't disappoint LeBeau, the man they affectionately refer to as "Coach Dad."

"I don't know if there's anyone like him," said Pro Bowl safety Troy Polamalu. "He's awesome. He's the best."

LeBeau, 71, is in his 50th year of coaching in the NFL, 10 of which have been spent with the Steelers. Since returning for his second tour of duty in 2004, the Steelers defense has finished No. 1 in the league three times—2004, 2007, and 2008—and never ranked lower than No. 9.

"It's kind of like a big brother or father figure up there teaching you the way and you want to make sure you make him proud," said cornerback Deshea Townsend. "That's why we go out and play so hard."

"He treats the last guy on the team like the first guy on the team," inside linebacker Larry Foote said. "He treats Pro Bowlers and free agents the same way. I want to get into coaching one day, not at this level, at the high school level, but I definitely want to model myself after him, his style."

LeBeau still runs the zone-blitz defense he helped devise and conceptualize with defensive coordinator Dom Capers when Bill Cowher brought him in as the secondary coach in 1992. It is built on speed, aggression, and deception, and it can be so confusing that opposing quarterbacks would have an easier time trying to solve a Rubik's Cube.

Just look at the passer ratings of five quarterbacks who faced the Steelers this season: Baltimore's Joe Flacco (22.2), New England's Matt Cassel (39.4), San Diego's Philip Rivers, the NFL passing leader (44.4), Dallas' Tony Romo (44.9), and Washington's Jason Campbell (49.2).

That doesn't even count Cleveland's Bruce Gradkowski, who finished with a 1.0 rating, nearly becoming the 10th quarterback in NFL history to finish with the Blutarski-esque 0.0 rating. And the Steelers were able to do that despite playing four games without Townsend and six without cornerback Bryant McFadden and defensive end Brett Keisel because of injuries.

"I don't think there's any coach in the business who can scheme like he schemes and game-plan like he does," said inside linebacker James Farrior, who, at age 33, was selected to his second Pro Bowl. "His wisdom and knowledge of the game gives him a great advantage over teams and over coaches. I don't see anybody outfox him." ■

Le'Ron McClain is corralled by linebacker Larry Foote (50) and defensive tackle Casey Hampton (98) during the second half of the game in Baltimore in December 2008.

Defense Reigns

Cassel rocked as Harrison and company take out decade of frustration with wet victory

Steelers 33, Patriots 10 • Sunday, Nov. 30, 2008 • By Ed Bouchette

New England's days of NFL domination ended a while back, either in the past Super Bowl or, for sure, when the Patriots lost Tom Brady in the season opener. Their reign over the Steelers also came to a brutal, wet, and cold end. It was as if the Steelers took out a decade of frustration on the Patriots, crushing them 33–10 in a hard, wintry New England rain.

For the first time in 11 years, the Steelers won here—and for only the second time in their past eight games. "It's a big monkey off our backs," said Steelers receiver Hines Ward, in his 11ᵗʰ season. "It seems like the Patriots have just been whipping our tails since I've been here."

They did until yesterday.

The Steelers' vicious defense turned extra mean on a Pittsburgh kind of afternoon. New England quarterback Matt Cassel was sacked five times, with linebacker James Harrison forcing fumbles on two of them, and he was intercepted twice. And safety Ryan Clark hit Patriots wide receiver Wes Welker so hard that up in Boston they may have thought the British were coming again.

"We haven't won here in years," said second-year linebacker LaMarr Woodley, a 13-year-old in Michigan the previous time the Steelers won at New England, 1997. "To come out here and get a win like this feels great."

Not only did they beat New England, the Steelers welcomed back their running game, and Ben Roethlisberger threw two touchdown passes. Willie Parker started at halfback and combined with Mewelde Moore to help the Steelers to 161 yards rushing, their highest total since the second game of the season. "It's just great to come out and beat them at their place and beat them the way we did," Parker said.

Roethlisberger completed 17 of 33 passes in the rain for 179 yards with one interception. He was sacked just once, on a corner blitz, and threw touchdown passes of 19 yards to Santonio Holmes and 11 to Hines Ward. Jeff Reed made four of his five field-goal attempts.

The only time it looked like a typical Steelers-Patriots game came early when linebacker Mike Vrabel intercepted Roethlisberger's second pass at the Steelers' 14. Three plays later, Sammy Morris ran over the left side from 2 yards out and the Patriots had a 7–0 lead.

"Vrabel, he's a heck of a player, and he made a great play on it," Roethlisberger said.

Roethlisberger bounced back, though. He led the Steelers on a 62-yard drive after Holmes returned a punt 29 yards. They had to settle for a Reed 20-yard field goal. Stephen Gostkowski put the Patriots on top, 10–3, with a 29-yard field goal with 6:48 left in the second quarter.

It was the Patriots' last hurrah.

The Steelers tied it with 1:55 left in the half on Roethlisberger's 19-yard scoring pass to Holmes. The Patriots moved the ball well to open the second half too, reaching a second-and-1 at the Steelers' 31.

Though this pass fell incomplete, New England's Matt Cassel had trouble keeping passes away from the Pittsburgh defenders. The Steelers intercepted him twice, leading directly to 10 Steelers points.

However, Casey Hampton pushed up the middle to sack Cassel and New England came up empty.

The Steelers responded with a drive that carried 79 yards on 14 plays but settled for a 25-yard field goal by Reed that put them ahead for good, 13–10. Their next possession turned out more profitable.

New England muffed the ensuing kickoff and Keyaron Fox recovered for the Steelers at the New England 8. Two plays later, Roethlisberger hit Ward at the 1, and he powered his way into the end zone for an 11-yard touchdown reception and a 20–10 Steelers lead.

Lightning on this rainy day struck again for the Steelers five seconds later. New England set up shop at its 29 after the kickoff and on first down, Harrison beat tackle Matt Light around the corner and stripped Cassel of the football for a sack and a fumble that was recovered by Woodley at the 26. The Steelers again could not get into the end zone, but Reed made it 23–10 with his third field goal, this one from 20 yards.

Harrison had another strip-and-sack of Cassel late in the third quarter but Reed missed from 40 yards out, only his second miss of the season. "That's what we've come to expect from him because that's what he's capable of," Tomlin said of Harrison, who pulled within one sack of tying the team single-season record of 15. "He's got tremendous talent. He's got tremendous work ethic and he's a heck of a football player."

So is Pro Bowl safety Troy Polamalu, who came up with his sixth interception of the season, which led to another field goal and a 26–10 lead with 5:43 left to play. Linebacker Lawrence Timmons then returned an interception 89 yards to the New England 1, and Gary Russell plunged in from there for the final score with 2:44 left.

"It hasn't been much of a rivalry because they've gotten after us," said Steelers coach Mike Tomlin. "For it to be a rivalry, we've got to win some and that's what we set out to do when we came up here today." ■

(opposite) James Harrison was a thorn in the side of the New England blockers all day. He had two sacks, both of which forced fumbles. (above) Willie Parker was back in action, but Mewelde Moore was strong off the bench. He carried 12 times for 67 yards.

Big "D"
Defense rules the day versus Dallas

Steelers 20, Cowboys 13 · Sunday, Dec. 7, 2008 · By Ed Bouchette

A game-winning touchdown, four turnovers, and three sacks sum up a totalitarian performance by the Pittsburgh defense. The game tied, Dallas had the ball on its 17 with 1:51 to go, and Steelers coach Mike Tomlin called a time out?

"Did you all really call a time out?" Cowboys quarterback Tony Romo yelled across the line to the Steelers' LaMarr Woodley and James Farrior.

"Yeah, what's your problem?" Farrior responded. "I don't know what else he thought would happen. That definitely added little fuel to the fire."

And on his next play, Romo and the Cowboys imploded. Steelers cornerback Deshea Townsend picked off an overthrown pass and ran it back 25 yards for a touchdown with 1:40 left that gave the Steelers an improbable 20–13 comeback victory against the Cowboys at Heinz Field.

The Steelers scored 17 points in the final 7:15 to come from 13–3 down to run their record to 10–3. It ended appropriately on a day in which the Steelers defense kept handing its offense opportunities only to see them squandered.

"Those guys fought, they believed in one another, and they didn't blink in the face of adversity, most of which was caused by us," Tomlin said.

The Steelers offense, stopped at the goal line early in the fourth quarter, finally broke through when Jeff Reed kicked his second field goal, from 41 yards, with 7:15 left to put them within 13–6.

Roethlisberger, who had a terrible first half and was sacked five times, then strung together a 67-yard drive, mainly by completing three passes to Nate Washington for 51 yards. He scrambled for an important 9 yards and made the first down by half the length of the football on a fourth-and-inches sneak. Heath Miller tied the game, 13–13, when he caught a 6-yard touchdown pass from Roethlisberger with 2:04 left.

Fortunately for the Steelers, the Cowboys were having as many problems on offense, if not more. Tony Romo completed 19 of 36 passes for 210 yards and one third-quarter touchdown pass of 12 yards to Terrell Owens to go with two Nick Folk field goals. But Romo was intercepted three times and lost a fumble, among the five Dallas turnovers.

Roethlisberger was 17 of 33 for 204 yards and lost a fumble on a quarterback sneak, but he was not intercepted and he came up big on the tying-touchdown drive.

It was the 16th game in which the Steelers under Roethlisberger have won in the final period when tied or behind. "It just seems like he tends to grow a cape," offensive tackle Willie Colon said. "We kind of feed off him."

Both offenses stunk in the first half to the point where it may have been more entertaining to just let the two defenses play each other. The Steelers gained 89 yards and lost two fumbles—one on what would have been a successful fourth-and-1 sneak by Roethlisberger, the other after a catch and fumble by Miller.

The Dallas defense played well in Pittsburgh, limiting the Steelers offense. Hines Ward did not make this catch and was limited to just one grab for two yards in the game.

The Cowboys gained 134 yards and committed four turnovers–interceptions of Romo by Troy Polamalu and Ike Taylor, a fumble by Romo on another sack by James Harrison, his 15th of the season, and a muffed punt. Despite those four Cowboys turnovers, the Steelers managed only three points.

Roethlisberger was dreadful in the first half–6 of 18 for 63 yards and that lost fumble. The Steelers offense wasted Polamalu's interception that ended Dallas' first series, with a drive that ended with Reed's 45-yard field goal try wide right.

The Steelers defense was heroic in the first half, twice stopping fourth-down thrusts by Dallas to go along with those two interceptions and forced fumble. But the Cowboys tied the score on the final play of the first half, then took the lead on their first drive of the second.

The Steelers offense looked to be on its last legs when Roethlisberger and Santonio Holmes breathed some life into it. They hooked up on a 47-yard pass from their 20 on third-and-long.

"It was just a big, big play at an appropriate time," Tomlin said. "Third-and-16 under those conditions,

based upon what we had done through that point in the game, was a dire situation. It was big-time protection, a big-time throw, and a big-time catch."

They moved to a first down at the five, but did not score. Gary Russell got the call on the next play and was tackled for a 2-yard loss and the Steelers turned it over to the Cowboys at the 3. There was 12:20 left in the game and the Dallas defense celebrated as if it were over.

"I just told the guys the game is not over, it's not close to over," said Farrior, the defensive captain.

The defense held field position at the 18 and the offense got another shot when Holmes returned a low punt 35 yards to the Dallas 25. The Steelers barely made it count after Roethlisberger was sacked back to the 23 on third down and Reed kicked a 41-yard field goal. It did bring Pittsburgh to within one score, however, and they made the next one count, driving 67 yards to tie it on Miller's touchdown catch.

That set up Townsend's dramatic interception. "We wanted to get our offense the ball back," Townsend said.

They did that too, with 51 seconds left, and they ran out the clock. ∎

(opposite) The Steelers were credited with 26 rushes in the game but averaged just 2.7 yards per carry. Mewelde Moore finished with 22 yards on five carries. (above) Willie Parker again carried the bulk of the load, but against Dallas it meant just 12 carries for 25 yards—a 2.1 yards-per-carry average.

Dividing Line

Holmes' score clinches AFC North

Steelers 13, Ravens 9 • Sunday, Dec. 14, 2008 • By Ed Bouchette

You can page through Steelers history and find all kinds of dramatic victories, important victories, aesthetically pleasing victories, and bigger comebacks. Few regular-season games will rank above this one at M&T Bank Stadium, when the Steelers' No. 26-ranked offense scored the only touchdown of the game with 43 seconds left to end a 92-yard drive against the league's No. 2 defense, pull out a 13–9 victory, and win the AFC North Division title and a first-round playoff bye.

That it came against their heated rivals on their field in a rough-and-tumble game and ended on a disputed 4-yard touchdown pass from Ben Roethlisberger to Santonio Holmes only enhanced the flavor.

"Boy, we have an excited football team in that room next door," Steelers coach Mike Tomlin said just outside his locker room. "Rightfully so. That was a ridiculously tough football game." It was the second late comeback victory in a row for the Steelers, who scored 17 points in the final 7:14 to beat the Cowboys last week. "Hopefully," Tomlin said, "that was the signature of Steelers football for '08."

The 92-yard drive staved off a defeat that would have locked the Steelers in a tie with Baltimore atop the division and a possible wild-card playoff berth. Instead, they clinched at least the No. 2 seed and a week off after the season before they would begin the playoffs at Heinz Field. And a win the following week against Tennessee would give them the inside track to the top seed.

"It's a good day," said Hines Ward, who caught eight passes for 107 yards and was among those wearing an AFC North championship hat in the locker room. "I'm going to wear it tonight, but there's a bigger picture. I want a Super Bowl."

That drive, and another outstanding defensive performance, put them in a prime position to seek that goal.

The Steelers' offense moved in fits and spurts and did not finish, settling for two short Jeff Reed field goals until they started the winning drive at the 8 with 3:36 left and trailing, 9–6. It took 12 plays, 11 of them passes including a spike to kill the clock. Roethlisberger completed seven of them for 89 yards.

"Seven [Roethlisberger] delivered, as he's done time and time again," Tomlin said. "I think a lot has been said about our offensive struggles, particularly in the last several weeks. One thing that is consistent is that when we need plays, when we have to move the ball, we have."

Holmes caught the final one on third down, as Roethlisberger rolled left, thought about running, then stopped and fired to his right. Holmes caught it with both feet in the end zone but the officials first ruled the ball did not break the plane and spotted it just short of the goal line. After viewing the replay, they changed their minds and ruled it a touchdown.

"I didn't know how that was going to turn out," said Holmes, who redeemed himself after muffing a punt and dropping a pass earlier. "I was really happy

Upended on this play, Willie Parker again led the Steelers in carries, despite being banged up. He went for 47 yards on 14 carries as the Steelers swept the Ravens for the first time since 2002.

when they gave me the touchdown, but I think we would have scored on the next play anyway."

Said Baltimore linebacker Ray Lewis, "We lost the game, that's the bottom line. There aren't any freaking excuses...of course, he didn't get in, but they called it the way they called it."

Tomlin gave no clue afterward whether he would have gone for the touchdown to win it there or kicked a field goal to send it to overtime. But, as he said, it did not matter.

Until the Steelers put together the winning drive, both defenses were as advertised, No. 1 and No. 2 in the league and vicious. The difference before the drive was three field goals by Baltimore's Matt Stover, two by Reed.

"We wanted to come in here and shut down their running game," Steelers linebacker James Harrison.

"That was really important to us."

They did not quite do that because Le'Ron McClain gained 87 yards and the Ravens had 112 total, on 31 carries. That edged the Steelers' ground game of 91 yards on 27 carries, led by Willie Parker's 47 on 14.

But Ravens rookie quarterback Joe Flacco had the toughest game of all. He completed just 11 of 28 passes for 115 yards, was sacked twice, and threw two interceptions, one early to Ryan Clark and one by William Gay that ended Baltimore's desperation drive at the end.

"Persevering and pushing through, whether it's a great defense, the weather, struggles, whatever it is, we found a way to get it done," said Roethlisberger, who completed 22 of 40 passes for 246 yards, one touchdown, and no interceptions. ∎

(opposite) Hines Ward returned to the forefront of the Pittsburgh passing attack after a poor game against Dallas, catching eight balls for 107 yards. (above) This touchdown catch by Santonio Holmes was one of the most pivotal plays in the Steelers' season.

Second Fiddle

With a top seed in the AFC on the line, Steelers fall flat and are manhandled by the No. 1 Titans

Titans 31, Steelers 14 · Sunday, Dec. 21, 2008 · By Ed Bouchette

The Steelers searched for their conference's No. 1 playoff seed and instead the Tennessee Titans planted them. The final verdict came in at 31–14, the worst loss of 2008 for the Steelers, who ended the meaningful portion of their season with an 11 4 record, the No. 2 seed, and a meaningless game awaiting them against Cleveland at Heinz Field.

Their five-game winning streak ended rudely with Titans gleefully stomping and wiping their noses on Terrible Towels at LP Field as Tennessee claimed the AFC's top playoff seed.

"They were the best team in the AFC today," Steelers safety Ryan Clark said. "Obviously, you have to come through here now. That's what today was all about."

The victory was complete for the Titans (12–2). They ran for 117 yards and two touchdowns against the league's No. 2 rush defense, became the first team to gain 300 yards against that defense this season, and sacked Steelers quarterback Ben Roethlisberger five times, forcing him to fumble four times (losing two). Titans safety Michael Griffin intercepted him twice, returning one for an 83-yard touchdown with 16 seconds left.

Even normally reliable kicker Jeff Reed missed a 33-yard field-goal attempt.

"They came out, they ran the ball, they threw the ball, they played defense," Clark said "They were an unbelievable team today, and we did nothing to stop them."

Tennessee quarterback Kerry Collins completed 20 of 29 for 216 yards, one touchdown, and no interceptions, becoming the only quarterback to ring up a 100 passer rating against the Steelers' defense this season. He was sacked just once, by James Harrison—Harrison's team-record 16th—as the Steelers failed to apply much pressure to the 35-year-old former Penn State quarterback.

Roethlisberger completed 26 of 40 for 331 yards and touchdowns of 31 yards to Santonio Holmes and 21 to Hines Ward in the second and third quarters that temporarily put the Steelers in front, 14–10. But he was under a heavy rush, did not protect the ball, and again got little help from his running game.

"Today wasn't one of our better performances," said Ward, who led all receivers with 109 yards on seven receptions.

The Steelers managed a mere 71 yards rushing with Willie Parker gaining only 29 on 18 carries—six of those for losses and three other carries for no gain. They set a negative tone early when they had a first down at the Tennessee 3 on their second possession. Parker hit right guard for a 1-yard loss, hit right tackle for 3 more yards in losses, and then Roethlisberger lost a fumble while scrambling that the Titans recovered at their 5.

"When you defend a short field and you get out of a red zone situation and don't give up any points, it's uplifting not only for a defense, but for a football team," Steelers coach Mike Tomlin said.

The Tennessee defense was stingy against the run all day. Mewelde Moore recorded 22 yards on his three carries, but the Steelers as a whole were held to 74 yards on the ground.

The Titans took that emotional lift and ran to a 10–0 second-quarter lead on a 42-yard Rob Bironas field goal and a 34-yard touchdown pass from Collins to Justin Gage after another lost Roethlisberger fumble two plays later.

"I didn't play well," Roethlisberger said. "Obviously, I'm never one to shy away from taking the blame, but that's a great football team. Whether it was their pass rush or their secondary, they're a great football team and they made plays all over the field."

The Steelers, though, did not wilt at that point and came back on Roethlisberger's two touchdown passes. Holmes made a nice diving catch of the first in the second quarter. Ward caught his at the 5 and took a big hit from cornerback Cortland Finnegan that helped him bounce into the end zone for a score. That put the Steelers in front 14–10 with 9:41 left in the third quarter, and the game started to look like a classic between the top two seeds.

The Titans reclaimed the lead in the third quarter on a 21-yard run by Chris Johnson, the longest touchdown run against the Steelers this season and only the fourth run of more than 20 yards. "We're not used to seeing that," defensive end Aaron Smith said. "They ran the ball very effectively against us today."

And the Steelers' offense kept giving them more chances. Five plays after Johnson's touchdown put Tennessee in front 17–14, Roethlisberger's pass for Nate Washington was picked off by Griffin.

Tennessee took over at the Steelers' 37. The Titans lined up to kick a field goal from their 4 on fourth down, but the officials penalized Chris Hoke for barking out "hut-hut" on defense. With a first down at the 2, it took LenDale White two 1-yard cracks to score on the first play of the fourth quarter. The lead was 10 points, and the Steelers never again threatened.

But it was not losing the top seed that bothered the Steelers as much as the way they did it. "I think losing the way we lost, the showing we did, sits with you longer than losing the No. 1 seed," Smith said. ∎

(opposite) Santonio Holmes provided the biggest highlight of the game with this stunning diving catch on a 31-yard pass from Roethlisberger. He finished with five catches for 93 yards. (above) Hines Ward made seven catches on the day, accounting for 109 of Roethlisberger's 329 passing yards and a touchdown. Unfortunately, Big Ben turned the ball over four times on the afternoon.

Lump & Thump

Roethlisberger's head injury puts big damper on easy victory against lowly Cleveland

Steelers 31, Browns 0 • Sunday, Dec. 28, 2008 • By Ed Bouchette

The Steelers used the lowly Cleveland Browns to triumphantly springboard into the playoffs, but not before their quarterback put a momentary lump in their throats when he was carted off the field just before the first half. But Ben Roethlisberger, who has made comebacks on and off the field a hallmark of his five-year career, likely will do it again. He was diagnosed with a concussion and "At this point, all tests are negative, which is positive," coach Mike Tomlin said.

That was the good news on one of the few pieces of bad news for the Steelers in their 31–0 thumping of the Browns, who finished one of their most disappointing seasons at 4–12 amid reports that accurately predicted coach Romeo Crennel would be fired.

The Steelers wrapped up one of their best regular seasons at 12–4 and felt their lopsided victory in what was a meaningless game to their playoff position would bode well for them when they open their run for the Super Bowl as the AFC's No. 2 seed.

"That was the exclamation point that we were looking for to end our regular season," Tomlin said. "Hopefully that momentum will prepare us for January football."

Not accounting for the opponent, the Steelers played their most dominant game of the season. Willie Parker had 116 yards of their 176 rushing, including the season's longest run from scrimmage, a 34-yard touchdown. The NFL's No. 1-ranked defense smothered Pittsburgh native Bruce Gradkowski and

his passing offense, holding it to 20 net yards. Things went so poorly for Gradkowski (5 of 16, 18 yards, 3 sacks) that his leading receiver was Steelers free safety Tyrone Carter. He intercepted two Gradowski passes and returned them a combined 50 yards, including one for 32 yards and a touchdown.

"It is great being out there again," said Carter, who started for injured Ryan Clark, "being part of a great win, not only for me but my teammates, as well as going into this playoff roll with a big win and carrying that momentum over to the next game."

It took a while for that momentum to build, in part because Roethlisberger was intercepted at the Browns' 6 in the first quarter and because his long touchdown pass to Nate Washington was negated by a holding penalty. Yet, once the spigots opened, they poured it on the Browns.

Parker, running behind a fullback in the I-formation far more than in any game this season, turned the corner around right end, slipped some grasps of a few Browns, and ran 34 yards into the end zone with 4:07 left in the first half for the game's initial score. The plan was to run, an order Tomlin issued a week before, and they did just that as Parker topped 100 for the first time since Nov. 16 against San Diego. "It was a good feeling knowing we were going to go out there and run it and it was up to their defense to stop it," Parker said. "Their defense didn't give up, we just had it in our mind-set we were going to run the ball and we just kept pounding."

Heath Miller was the Steelers' second-leading receiver in the easy win over Cleveland, picking up 55 yards on five catches.

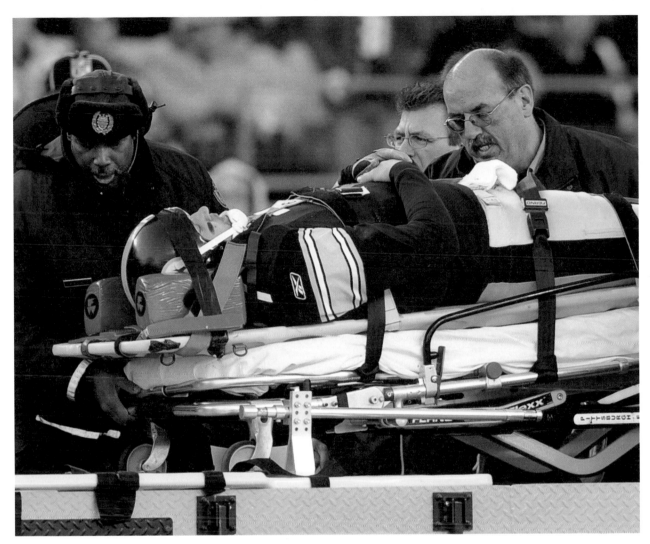

Roethlisberger was injured on the third play of the Steelers' next series when he was knocked to the surface by linebackers Willie McGinest and D'Qwell Jackson and his head bounced off the turf. Byron Leftwich completed the drive and, on third down, scrambled up the middle for 8 yards, a touchdown and a 14–0 lead 32 seconds before the half.

Carter got things going in the second half when he intercepted a pass after blitzing cornerback Bryant McFadden hit Gradkowski's arm. That led to Jeff Reed's 22-yard field goal. Gary Russell ended an 88-yard drive by running 3 yards for a touchdown and a 24–0 lead. A minute later, Carter intercepted a deflected pass and returned it 32 yards for the final score.

Hines Ward caught his 800th career pass from rookie quarterback Dennis Dixon in the fourth quarter and topped 1,000 yards receiving for the fifth time. But the game was more about the future than it was about the past, the future being the opening of the playoffs in Heinz Field..

"We feel like we can play with anyone," defensive end Brett Keisel said. "We've done a good job of putting us in position to make a run; now we just need to do it. We need to seize the opportunity and do it." ∎

(opposite) Before leaving the game due to injury and turning the reins over to Byron Leftwich, Ben Roethlisberger completed 9 of 14 passes for 110 yards and an interception. (above) Roethlisberger's head injury was one of the scariest moments of the NFL season, as he lay on the field for 15 minutes before being carted off. Luckily, he did not miss a start thanks to the team's bye week to begin the playoffs.

The Dynasty

Steelers' Rooney basking in super year

By Ed Bouchette

At the age of 76, Dan Rooney certainly has seen a lot and done plenty during his days that began in the Great Depression. His father, Art, founded a team in the National Football League and saw it become one of pro sports' dynasties in the 1970s. He and his father were inducted into the Pro Football Hall of Fame, and his team won five Super Bowls.

Nothing over the past three quarters of a century, though, can top the professional year Dan Rooney has been having right now.

Against long odds, he and his son Art II cobbled together new investors and financing during a terrible economy to keep in his family the Steelers, the franchise that *ESPN The Magazine* suggested is the best in pro sports. He became friendly with President Barack Obama, publicly endorsed him, and stumped for him heavily in the presidential campaign. And his team won its sixth Super Bowl.

Not a bad year, eh?

"It's been tremendous," said Dan Rooney, declaring it his best professional year, not counting all the family moments a father of nine and husband to Patricia for 58 years can have. "There's been no year as eventful."

The Steelers won their sixth Lombardi Trophy, the most by any team, against the Arizona Cardinals, a franchise that once played with them under the same banner—the combined Card-Pitt team of 1944. That concession to the football manpower shortage during World War II came one season after a similar combination with the Philadelphia Eagles, known as the Steagles. And those efforts followed Art Rooney Sr.'s selling his team briefly after the 1940 season.

Art Rooney Sr. later resisted many efforts to either move his team or sell it in the two subsequent decades. His son Dan did the same thing this past year. He helped persuade his four brothers not to take a more lucrative offer and to instead sell their shares to him, his son and team president Art Rooney II, and to new minority owners. Brothers Pat and Tim agreed to sell their ownership and brothers Art Jr. and John sold about half of their stake. Each had owned 16 percent of the team.

NFL owners approved the sale without a negative vote cast. Had it gone another way, Dan Rooney would not have been able to celebrate his team's victory in Super Bowl XLIII with such satisfaction.

"It meant a lot to me," he said with typical understatement.

He spoke about the early days of the franchise, how he remembered hanging around the team and attending games as early as age 5, when his father permitted it.

"It's easy to say I grew up with it," Rooney said. "What I am saying to you is, I was able to see as I did grow up and built on it, I was able to see what we do mean here. In tough times. This city has had tough times as we all know. And the team has been a real plus, something people had a real regard for.

Art Rooney, president of the Pittsburgh Steelers, right, poses with his son, Dan, general manager of the club, in Pittsburgh, in January 1966. Art Rooney Sr. was a skillful owner who treated his players as partners rather than employees.

"I looked at the situation, how our father started this team in 1933; it's not something we should just give up on. That was a real plus to be able to do that."

David Fleming, in his *ESPN The Magazine* piece, told of how he encountered Mr. Rooney on an elevator at Heinz Field after the AFC Championship Game. As fans crowded on as well, Rooney chatted with them. Many other team owners will not permit another soul—other than the kind of bodyguards Rooney never has—to step on the same elevator with them.

In the Steelers' cafeteria, which is also open to the UPMC health care professionals on the South Side campus, Rooney often stands in line behind office workers, trainers, and even some in the media

to order his food.

So, yes, keeping the Steelers in the family "meant a lot" to him.

His football team was a bit of an underdog this season. It had the NFL's toughest schedule and injuries hit the Steelers early.

"We had a great season, a tremendous season," Rooney said. "Everybody, including the NFL I might add, said we had the toughest schedule in football and it sure looked that way. Then we had a 12–4 season, which is a real tribute to [head coach] Mike Tomlin. Then we got into the playoffs and we're going to the Super Bowl."

It may be routine for the Steelers, who have been

(opposite) Democratic presidential hopeful, Senator Barack Obama, D-Ill. walks with Pittsburgh Steelers Chairman Dan Rooney on April 14, 2008, at the David Lawrence Convention Center in Pittsburgh. (above) Rooney stands with his presenter, Joe Greene, after Rooney was enshrined in the Pro Football Hall of Fame in July 2000 in Canton, Ohio.

to seven Super Bowls and now won six of them, but it's not old hat to the owner.

"Noooo," Rooney said. "I remember looking at this in 2005. You look at the situation where you have young people, new players coming along and getting better and more confidence and you can see them playing together and it develops. I think that's the big thing. It never does get old. You always have a new situation. These are new players when you consider there's less than half of the players who were with us in 2005. And we have a new coach."

Tomlin, in his second season, is only the third Steelers head coach in the past 40 years. Chuck Noll won four Super Bowls in 23 seasons, Bill Cowher one in 15 seasons. Rooney called all three "great coaches," but surely they also had the good fortune to join the organization with him running the show.

"I will say that we have a certain standard," Rooney said. "Guys come in and they get into the program and they see; it's basically how we operate. We believe in operating the right way, we believe in trying to do things the way they should be. We try to take players, draft players, sign players in a professional, fair way. And so I think the coach, the last three particularly, fits into that mold."

It's been some kind of year for Dan Rooney. On Super Bowl Sunday it became even better. ∎

(opposite) Rooney holds up the Vince Lombardi Trophy after the Steelers' Super Bowl XL win over the Seattle Seahawks on February 5, 2006. (above) Rooney accepts the AFC Championship trophy from former Steeler Rod Woodson as broadcaster Jim Nantz looks on after the Steelers defeated the Ravens 23–14 on January 18, 2009.

Many Happy Returns

Heinz Field will be the site of the AFC Championship Game for a third time

Steelers 35, Chargers 24 · Sunday, Jan. 12, 2009 · By Ed Bouchette

The Steelers will play their third AFC Championship Game at Heinz Field this decade, and this time they would like to win. To do so, they must get past their mirror images, the Baltimore Ravens, who not only play like them but are trying to emulate what the Steelers did after the 2005 season as the wild-card No. 6 seed.

"What else would you expect?" Steelers coach Mike Tomlin said. "Us and the Ravens; it would be a big game if it was a scrimmage. It just happens to be the AFC Championship Game."

The Steelers became the only home team of the weekend's four playoff games to win when they defeated San Diego 35–24 with a withering third quarter in which the Chargers were allowed just one play. That play became a Larry Foote interception.

"I think we played our kind of football today," Tomlin said after his first playoff victory.

It was old-school Steelers football, harkening back to the days when they won playoff games at home in the 1970s. Their defense might not have a fancy nickname, but it did 2 yards better than the Steel Curtain that held the Minnesota Vikings to 17 yards rushing in Super Bowl IX. The Steelers yesterday held the Chargers to 15 yards, a club postseason record.

"It was big," linebacker LaMarr Woodley said after the defense held Darren Sproles to 15 yards on 11 carries. "We definitely didn't want to get him going."

And there was the return of their own ground game. Willie Parker ran for two touchdowns and 146 yards, the most in a playoff game since Franco Harris had 153 against the Baltimore Colts in 1975. Quarterback Ben Roethlisberger showed no signs of a two-week-old concussion. He completed 17 of 26 passes for 181 yards and threw a touchdown pass of 8 yards to Heath Miller. Roethlisberger was sacked just once as the line gave him plenty of time to throw.

"I can't say enough about the Steelers," San Diego coach Norv Turner said. "They are an outstanding football team."

The top-ranked Steelers defense did a good job of getting to Rivers and hit him a number of times. "The fact that he did get hit and sacked may have thrown off his timing," linebacker James Harrison said. "And the illusion of pressure—pressure that's not actually there because you are used to getting hit every three or four seconds." They sacked the Chargers' quarterback four times, two by Woodley, to go with Foote's interception off a deflected pass by end Brett Keisel.

No play, though, was bigger than the Steelers' first punt return of the season for a touchdown. It was also the longest in the team's playoff history. The return came after San Diego shocked the Steelers by scoring on four plays in the game's first series. Rivers hit Vincent Jackson with a 41-yard touchdown pass that was pulled in over Ike Taylor in the end zone.

The raucous Heinz Field crowd turned quietly anxious after that lightning-bolt score against the NFL's

Former Super Bowl MVP Hines Ward is one of the biggest stars in the NFL come playoff time. He had yet another strong outing in the divisional round against San Diego, a game where he caught four passes for 70 yards.

best defense. But then, on came Santonio Holmes. He fielded a booming Mike Scifres punt midway through the opening quarter at the Steelers' 33, made one cut to avoid the first rush, another to get outside, and a final leap over a defender to run 67 yards for a touchdown that tied the score and breathed life back into the crowd and—if they'll admit it—his teammates.

"It was great; it sparked this team," Holmes said. "The crowd was behind us 100 percent from then on. It was the play that we needed. After that our team just rallied behind [it] and put it to them."

Other than a failed fake punt that led to a San Diego field goal, it was all Steelers from that punt return until the middle of the fourth quarter. The Steelers lined up to punt with a little more than five minutes to go in the first half from their 48, a yard short of a first down. Instead of punting, they snapped it directly to Ryan Clark, lined up as a blocking back. The play, the first fake punt in Tomlin's two seasons as coach, lost 4 yards and the Chargers took over at the Steelers' 44. They drove 20 yards and Nate Kaeding kicked a 42-yard field goal with 1:56 left in the half to give San Diego a 10–7 lead.

"I was going to be aggressive," Tomlin explained. "I want our football team to know that I have a great deal of belief in them and that we are not going to play scared, we are going to play to win."

That belief manifested itself in a barrage of Steelers points. Parker scored on a 3-yard touchdown run with 40 seconds left in the half to give the Steelers a 14–10 lead. They drove 66 yards on seven plays to take their first lead of the game. Before Parker scored on a toss to the left, Hines Ward caught a 41-yard pass that carried to the San Diego 3.

Their next drive of the game, at the start of the second half, produced another touchdown. Behind Parker the Steelers ground out 77 yards on 13 plays. Miller caught Roethlisberger's 8-yard pass for a touchdown that put the Steelers in front 21–10.

The only time San Diego had the ball in the third quarter, besides returning kickoffs, came after Sproles returned a kickoff 63 yards to the Steelers' 23. On first down, Keisel tipped Rivers' pass and Foote intercepted at the 21.

The Steelers added another touchdown on Gary Russell's 1-yard run early in the fourth quarter for a 28–10 lead. San Diego pulled to within 28-17 when Rivers threw a 4-yard touchdown pass to Legedu Naanee with 9:09 left, capping a 73-yard, 10-play drive. But the Steelers responded with another scoring drive of 73 yards with Parker putting the exclamation point on his first 100-yard playoff game with a 16-yard touchdown run with 4:11 left.

Now another AFC Championship Game comes to Pittsburgh. The Steelers lost two previous games at Heinz Field to the Patriots after the 2001 and 2004 seasons. They also lost two out of three title games in Three Rivers Stadium in the 1990s. As Tomlin said though, "This is the story of the 2008 Pittsburgh Steelers."

They, not history, will get to write their own ending. ■

(opposite) San Diego's Eric Weddle was guilty of pass interference on Nate Washington during this play. The penalty went for 44 yards and set up Gary Russell's one-yard touchdown run. (above) Hines Ward and the Steelers were excited to be heading back to the AFC Championship Game, especially after a weekend that saw three of the four road teams in the NFL claim victories.

Heinz Finally Super

Polamalu's interception return for a touchdown in the fourth quarter punches Steelers' ticket

Steelers 23, Ravens 14 · Sunday, Jan. 18, 2009 · By Ed Bouchette

On a cold, snowy night, the sun finally shone on the Steelers in a championship game at Heinz Field. Safety Troy Polamalu ended a rolling Baltimore comeback when he intercepted a pass by rookie quarterback Joe Flacco and returned it 40 yards for a touchdown with 4:34 left to secure the Steelers' 23–14 victory against the Baltimore Ravens.

The victory, their first in a championship game on their third try at Heinz Field, lifted the Steelers into their seventh Super Bowl and provides them with a chance to become the first team to win six. Their seven AFC championships are a record. Their victory set off a jubilant celebration at eight-year-old Heinz Field, where the Lamar Hunt Trophy was presented to Dan Rooney and his son and team president Art Rooney, coach Mike Tomlin, and his players before a home crowd for the first time in 13 years.

Tomlin is the first Steelers coach to reach a Super Bowl in his second season.

The Steelers play against an unlikely opponent, the Arizona Cardinals, in Super Bowl XLIII. in Tampa, Fla. The Cardinals, often called "Pittsburgh West" because of their many connections to the city and the Steelers, will play in their first Super Bowl.

"We didn't start this journey to get to Tampa," Tomlin said on the field after the game to loud cheers from fans, most of whom stuck around for the trophy presentation and broke out in Steelers fight songs. "We are excited about being in the Super Bowl. We look forward to getting down there and pursuing our ultimate goals."

Before Polamalu's touchdown, that record crowd of 65,350 watched anxiously as the Ravens moved from their 12 to a first down at their 32, needing only a field goal to win. Flacco's pass was intended for Derrick Mason. It came from the Baltimore 29 after linebacker LaMarr Woodley's second sack of the game and it came as linebacker James Harrison hit Flacco. As a result, the ball did not come close to its target. Polamalu, the five-time Pro Bowl safety with seven interceptions in the regular season, caught the ball and then weaved to his right, moving through traffic. As he neared the end zone, he held the ball aloft in both hands as if offering it up to the gods.

"That's Troy," quarterback Ben Roethlisberger said. "He comes out of nowhere."

The Steelers never trailed, but the Ravens kept it close after falling behind 13–0 in the second quarter, and the Steelers helped them with some mental and physical mistakes.

Jeff Reed kicked two of his three field goals—from 34 and 42 yards—in the first quarter and Santonio Holmes turned a short pass into a 65-yard scoring play for that Steelers lead. However, Willis McGahee scored on a 3-yard run near the end of the half to make it 13–7.

Reed's 46-yard, third-quarter field goal stretched the lead to 16–7, but the Ravens closed the gap to 16–14 on McGahee's second touchdown, from the 1,

The Steelers were all smiles after one of the hardest-hitting games in recent NFL history. Willie Parker led the Steelers with 47 blue-collar yards, picked up over 24 carries with a long run of just seven yards.

with 9:29 left. McGahee later was carted off with what appeared to be a concussion after a hit by Ryan Clark.

Roethlisberger completed 16 of 33 passes for 255 yards with that touchdown to Holmes and no interceptions. Flacco threw three interceptions on his way to completing just 13 of 30 for 141 yards and a passer rating of just 18.2.

Neither team had much luck running the football. The Steelers managed only 52 yards on 28 carries, while Baltimore had 73 on 25.

The Steelers jumped out quickly. Hines Ward, who left the game in the second quarter with a knee injury, caught a 45-yard pass on the opening drive that carried to the Baltimore 23, but the Steelers settled for Reed's 34-yard field goal and a 3–0 lead. Reed made it two field goals on the first three drives when he kicked one from 42 yards with 6:11 to go in the first quarter for a 6–0 lead after a Deshea Townsend interception.

The Steelers, though, blew two big chances to go on top by 10 points on that series. Willie Parker broke wide open on a pass route at the 17 and dropped Roethlisberger's pass. Then, from the 24, Roethlisberger threw a perfect pass to Holmes at the 2. It was ruled a catch but after Ravens coach John Harbaugh challenged the play, it was overturned to an incomplete pass.

Parker later fumbled at his 43, but the Steelers defense rose to snuff the Ravens on third-and-1 and fourth-and-1. The Steelers took over at their 34 and three plays later it was 13–0. Roethlisberger stepped up and away from pressure on third down, moved to his left, and floated a pass to his right. Holmes caught the pass to the inside at Baltimore's 47. Holmes made his way to the left, then raced down the sideline and jumped for the pylon at the front of the end zone for a 65-yard score.

Roethlisberger said he was about to throw the ball away when he spotted Holmes. "I just threw it where he could make a play," Roethlisberger said. "You get him the ball, he'll do the rest."

The Ravens caught some lightning near the end of

(opposite) With the Ravens still lurking within striking distance and trailing by two points, Troy Polamalu sealed the Steelers trip to Tampa by returning a Joe Flacco pass 40 yards for a touchdown. (above) Santonio Holmes leaps for the goal line at the end of his 65-yard touchdown reception that saw him race down the sideline without stepping out of bounds. Holmes only had two catches in the game but made the most of his opportunities.

the half to keep it from being an early runaway. Jim Leonhard returned a punt 45 yards to the Steelers' 17. On third down from the 16, cornerback Bryant McFadden was flagged for pass interference against Mason at the 3. McGahee then scored standing up to pull the Ravens to within 13–7 with 2:40 left in the half.

And mistakes by the Steelers—physical and mental—just kept coming. Steelers rookie receiver Limas Sweed dropped what would have been a 50-yard touchdown pass at the 10 when he was wide open with just under a minute left in the first half. He then rolled around as if injured, costing the Steelers a precious timeout, their last of the half.

"I wish he'd just catch the football," Tomlin said. "That's all part of growing up."

The Steelers quickly moved to a first down at the 21, but with 16 seconds to go, Roethlisberger threw from the shotgun over the middle to Mewelde Moore. He was tackled at the 12 and before the Steelers could line up and spike the ball to stop the clock time ran out and so did the Steelers' chances to kick a field goal. "I

accept responsibility for that," Tomlin said.

Reed, though, did get his third field goal and it was a big one, from 46 yards with 3:38 left in the third quarter. It put the Steelers up by two scores, 16–7. Two key pass completions salvaged that 51-yard drive. The first was a 20-yard catch over the middle by Carey Davis on third down. The other was a 30-yard catch by Heath Miller on second-and-24.

Mistakes, though, continued to dog the Steelers. Berger struck again when he shanked a low punt 21 yards to give Baltimore a first down at its 42. After a James Harrison sack, Mason caught a 14-yard pass against cornerback Ike Taylor. The Ravens moved to a first down at the 24. Two plays later, Taylor was called for pass interference against Marcus Smith in the end zone, giving the Ravens a first down at the 1. McGahee ran around right end for his second touchdown and Baltimore was within two points with 9:29 left.

Polamalu's interception and weaving return for a touchdown put an end to that comeback and earned the Steelers their ticket to the Super Bowl. ∎

(opposite) When all was said and done, a familiar headline ran across the special editions of the Post-Gazette *distributed on the field: the Steelers were heading back to the Super Bowl. (above) With Dan Rooney and Mike Tomlin looking on, Willie Parker raises the Lamar Hunt Trophy, signifying the Steelers' rise over all challengers in the AFC.*

Troy Polamalu

A singular approach makes him doubly endearing

By Ron Cook

On the podium, in front of the prying world-wide Super Bowl media, with at least 10 television microphones about 2 inches from his face, Steelers safety Troy Polamalu was surprisingly smooth, every bit as at ease as when he took that interception back for a touchdown against the Baltimore Ravens a little more than a week before.

Off the podium later, during a brief walk to the Steelers hotel that provided a moment of quiet reflection so rare amid the big game hysteria, Polamalu made a fascinating pronouncement.

"I've never needed or wanted to be a red carpet A-lister."

Seconds later, Polamalu was engulfed by a throng of Steelers fans outside the hotel. Security tried to chase them away like flics, but a few got autographs, one or two a picture, one older woman even a hug.

So much for that quiet reflection.

So much for that A-lister business.

What a joy—an absolute joy—it is to watch Polamalu handle himself on sports' grandest stage. The quarterbacks in Super Bowl XLIII—the Steelers' Ben Roethlisberger and Arizona's Kurt Warner—are the brightest stars along with otherworldly wide receiver Larry Fitzgerald of the Cardinals. But Polamalu could be the biggest of all, if he chose to be. The extraordinary talent that has him going to his fifth Pro Bowl and, one day, barring injury, the Hall of Fame. The dark, throbbing good looks. That amazing hair.

Think of the endorsements out there! The money!

"I've done four or five commercials for Nike and one for Coke. That's it," Polamalu said, quietly, which is how he says everything.

Four or five seem about two dozen too few for an athlete of Polamalu's stardom, doesn't it? Not that it's surprising, though. The celebrity world still is a place where Polamalu isn't truly comfortable. This is a man who once said: "I don't like prestige. I could go off and live in the mountains and raise my family."

That was back in early 2006, not long after the Steelers beat Seattle in Super Bowl XL in Detroit. Polamalu loved sitting in the backseat then, watching the Jerome Bettis homecoming/farewell tour unfold. He'd prefer to take that same seat this week, but he knows that isn't possible because of his high-profile status in the game. He does better with the fame and is much better at handling the adulation that goes with it even if he fully realizes that so much of it is phony and for the wrong reasons.

If you asked Polamalu, he would tell you, flat out:

"Like and respect me because I'm a man of faith and a good family man, not because I'm pretty good at football."

Since that isn't going to happen...

"I deal with it," Polamalu said. "But I don't really like the attention. I mean, everybody likes it a little. But Monday through Saturday, I'd rather ensconce myself with my family."

And Sunday?

"Sundays are different," Polamalu said, grinning.

The Sunday against the Ravens, for instance.

Soft-spoken, introspective, and humble off the field, Troy Polamalu's demeanor belies an underlying tenacity that comes out in full force on the football field.

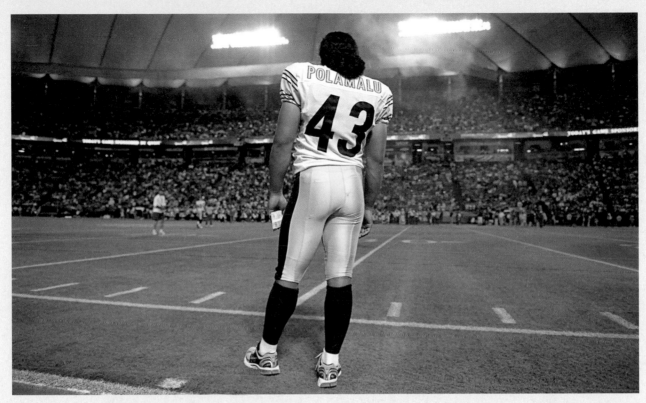

Polamalu sealed the deal in the Steelers' win in the AFC Championship Game by intercepting a Joe Flacco pass and returning it 40 yards for a touchdown. That play—rather, the image of Polamalu lugging the ball into the end zone and pointing skyward—was on the front page of this newspaper the next morning and many others across America.

Even Polamalu will agree that kind of attention is pretty cool because it usually means the Steelers win.

You should have heard him discussing the play, so calmly, so thoughtfully, so strategically. Many people tend to think of him as a free stylist in the Steelers' defense. That couldn't be further from the truth.

"I have responsibilities like everybody else," Polamalu said. "I was man-to-man with the tight end in the backfield. But when you have James Farrior, LaMarr Woodley, and James Harrison all blitzing, you know nobody probably is going to release. When you know your responsibility isn't going to be a threat, it allows you to free up and read the quarterback and make a play."

As Polamalu dropped into coverage, he noticed Flacco looking at wide receiver Derrick Mason. When he saw Flacco release the pass an instant before he wanted because of pressure from Harrison, he closed to the ball, made a leaping interception, then made that fabulous runback.

"We were already winning," Polamalu said when asked what it felt like to win such a big game.

That's the beautiful thing about Polamalu, that humility. Take Polamalu's observations about Cardinals safety Adrian Wilson: "If he were in our system, he'd probably do better than me. He's a better athlete. He's stronger and faster."

Yeah, right.

An eager interrogator asked Polamalu if he thought that his postseason performance elevated him to the pantheon of Steelers all-time defensive greats, the ones with names such as Greene and Lambert and Ham and Blount.

"I'm just another Steeler. Like anyone else," Polamalu said, dismissively.

His words were barely audible, but his pained look practically screamed:

You gotta be kidding me!"

Humility really is a beautiful thing.

Polamalu's humility, anyway. ■

(opposite) One of the best and hardest tacklers in the game, Polamalu has recorded 432 tackles, seven sacks, and 17 interceptions in his career. Beyond the stats, his ability to hit and be around nearly every play intimidates opponents into not taking risks they might take against other teams. (above) Already a two-time Super Bowl champion, Polamalu has also been named to five consecutive Pro Bowls, meaning he has been to Honolulu every season except for his rookie year.

Steeler Nation

Pittsburgh fans truly an army of one

By Robert Dvorchak

From Station Square to the space station, from Mount Washington to Mount Everest, from Polish Hill to the South Pole, Steelermania is at its peak. But it has never been a one-sided deal. From ownership on down to the practice squad, the Steelers want their vast and varied fan base to know that they are one with them in celebrating their record sixth Super Bowl championship.

"I feel that sometimes we're the heartbeat of the city," said defensive captain James Farrior. "They love us to death, and we love them the same way. We definitely feel like they're a part of this team also. They want to win as badly as we do."

After the Steelers punched their ticket to their seventh Super Bowl, Farrior was among the players seen taking a victory lap around Heinz Field. It wasn't a show of vanity, but a way to share the accomplishment with those who brave the snow and the cold, with those who watch and scream and risk their hearts for a football team.

"I definitely wanted to show my appreciation for what they've done," Farrior said. "It was the biggest crowd we ever had. That's the loudest I ever heard that stadium."

The bond between this team and its following is stronger than the strongest steel, a phenomenon worthy of sociological study. It is called The Nation, but it's more like an extended family or a tribal community that crosses political, religious, economic and worldly lines.

Combat troops in far away lands clutch the Terrible Towel to remind them of home. Jet jockeys take it with them on air patrols. And now it's gone otherworldly. Lt. Col. Mike Fincke of Emsworth smuggled a towel aboard a rocket ship and then claimed the International Space Station as Steeler Country.

There isn't enough canvas to make that large of a tent.

"It's just amazing to have such allegiance," said offensive lineman Max Starks. "I like to think we have the best fans in the entire sporting industry. You can go almost anywhere and there's a Steeler fan with a Terrible Towel somewhere, and now it's gone intergalactic."

The roots of this bond go back to the very beginnings of the game. A ledger entry from the Allegheny Athletic Association records a payment of $500 in 1892 to Pudge Heffelfinger to play in a game, and the Hall of Fame in Canton considers it to be the birth certificate of professional football.

The relationship really got hot when the Steelers started to win in the Super Seventies. "There were games when I thought if we didn't win, the fans were going to come down out of the stands and win it for us," said Andy Russell, defensive captain of the first two Super Bowl teams. "We have the best fans in the world. I've been in Steeler bars in Moscow."

Current players describe the relationship between the fans and the team as mutually beneficial to the point of being symbiotic. "We feed off them. They feed off of us. They're happy when we win, sad when we lose," said defensive lineman Brett Keisel. "Steeler

Nation is one of a kind, and I'm glad to be a part of it."

Teammate Aaron Smith has a personal and professional connection to the fan base. When his son was diagnosed with a rare form of leukemia, Pittsburghers turned out en masse to give their blood. "The city lives off of us," Smith said. "You know they're going to be behind you. This city takes care of its own. I can't imagine playing in a better city."

A fresh perspective can be supplied by those who have seen it from the outside and are now caught up in it. Quarterback Byron Leftwich, who began his career with the Jacksonville Jaguars, acknowledged with awe that Steeler fans can affect a game.

"I remember a game on a Sunday night or a Monday night when I was with Jacksonville. We were at home, and we had to use the silent count," he said. "Did y'all hear what I just said? We were in our own stadium, in Jacksonville, and there were so many Pittsburgh fans that we had to go on the quiet cadence like we were on the road," Leftwich added. "When you play for Pittsburgh, with the support we get from our fans, it's priceless. I'm just happy to be a part of it, to be on this kind of football team, to have the opportunity to win a Super Bowl."

"Everywhere we go, it's going to be a home game," said Hines Ward, the MVP of the last Super Bowl. "Our fans will take out a mortgage on the house to get there."

As Dan Rooney explained in his autobiography last year, the Steelers actually belong to the city of Pittsburgh, and his family merely shepherds the franchise. "Oh, yes, I believe that. Our fans are everything. That's why we're here. That's why it was so important for us to get our ownership structure worked out," said Mr. Rooney, who still walks to games from his family homestead on the North Side.

Affairs of the heart aren't readily explainable, but team president Arthur J. Rooney II, grandson of the franchise founder, relishes the boost the fans give his team. "It gives you goose hairs on the back of your neck, really, when you walk out onto the field and you're in a foreign city and you see all those Steeler fans and all those towels waving," he said. "There's no question I think it does inspire our players."

The players can attest to that, even those like linebacker LaMarr Woodley, who played in front of monster crowds at Michigan. "You definitely feed off the fans. It really says a lot about this team and about this city," he said. "They're not out there playing, but they're in the game with us. By making all that noise, they don't know how much that means to us."

Players who grew up in the Pittsburgh area note that economic hard times threw steelworkers out of a job and forced them to scatter to other areas, but their allegiance to the Steelers kept them connected to home. "Wherever we may play, our fans are already there, and their children became Steeler fans as well. The fan base around the country is unbelievable because of that reason," said Homestead native Charlie Batch, who was on injured reserve for the Super Bowl.

Ryan Mundy, a practice squad player, recalls that 15,000 people once showed up to see his Woodland Hills High School team win a triple overtime game over Central Catholic. It doesn't surprise him that Steelers fans have a sense of ownership in the team.

"They are a part of it. As a player, it's comforting and it's rewarding to know that so many people are behind you. That's great motivation for us. Not only do we want to win the Super Bowl for us, but for the fans," he said. "You'd have to look long and hard to find anything that matches this. We get pictures of guys serving in Iraq and Afghanistan or flying in jets showing off the Terrible Towel. That's very important to us," Mundy added. "That's why we're so selfless. We realize it's bigger than us. It'll always be bigger than us." ■

Stats

Team Statistics

	Steelers	Opponents
TOTAL FIRST DOWNS	290	240
FIRST DOWNS (Rushing-Passing-By Penalty)	93 - 179 - 18	73 - 149 - 18
THIRD DOWN CONVERSIONS	92/224	71/226
FOURTH DOWN CONVERSIONS	3/12	10/21
TOTAL OFFENSIVE YARDS	4991	3795
OFFENSE (Plays-Average Yards)	1015 - 4.9	974 - 3.9
TOTAL RUSHING YARDS	1690	1284
RUSHING (Plays-Average Yards)	460 - 3.7	390 - 3.3
TOTAL PASSING YARDS	3301	2511
PASSING (Comp-Att-Int-Avg)	303 - 506 - 15 - 7.1	301 - 533 - 20 - 5.4
SACKS	51	49
FIELD GOALS	27/31	24/27
TOUCHDOWNS	38	21
Rushing-Passing-Returns-Defensive	16 - 19 - 0 - 3	7 - 12 - 0 - 2
TIME OF POSSESSION (Avg/Game)	31:41	28:41
TURNOVER RATIO	+4	

Passing Statistics

Top Players	Att	Comp	Yds	Comp %	Yds/Att	TD	TD %	INT	INT %	Long	Sck	Sack/Lost	Rating
Ben Roethlisberger	469	281	3301	59.9	7.0	17	3.6	15	3.2	65	46	284	80.1
Byron Leftwich	36	21	303	58.3	8.4	2	5.6	0	0.0	50	3	22	104.3

Rushing Statistics

Top Players	Att	Yds	Yds/Att	Long	TD
Willie Parker	210	791	3.8	34	5
Mewelde Moore	140	588	4.2	32	5
Ben Roethlisberger	34	101	3.0	17	2
Gary Russell	28	77	2.8	15	3
Rashard Mendenhall	19	58	3.1	12	0
Carey Davis	12	35	2.9	11	0

Stats

Receiving Statistics

Top Players	Rec	Yds	Yds/Rec	Long	TD
Hines Ward	81	1043	12.9	49	7
Santonio Holmes	55	821	14.9	48	5
Heath Miller	48	514	10.7	22	3
Nate Washington	40	631	15.8	65	3
Mewelde Moore	40	320	8.0	25	1
Matt Spaeth	17	136	8.0	13	0

Defensive Statistics

Top Players	Tackles	Solo	Assists	Sacks	Fum Forced
James Farrior	133	87	46	4	1
James Harrison	101	67	34	16	7
Troy Polamalu	73	54	19	0	0
Ryan Clark	87	52	35	0	0
Ike Taylor	65	50	15	0	0
Aaron Smith	60	44	16	6	0
Lawrence Timmons	65	43	22	5	1
LaMarr Woodley	60	41	19	12	2
Bryant McFadden	41	37	4	1	0
Larry Foote	63	34	29	2	1
William Gay	41	33	8	0	0
Travis Kirschke	46	30	16	2	0
Brett Keisel	41	22	19	1	0

Pittsburgh Post-Gazette

TRIUMPH
BOOKS